COVENANT SEXUALITY:

ESSAYS ON RELIGION, SEXUALITY, AND IDENTITY

 Ezra Press

Published by Ezra Press

P.O. Box 9, STN Main, Grimsby,

Ontario, Canada L3M 4G1

Book design by Rachel Eras

Printed in the United States of America

ISBN: 978-1-989169-31-5

Contents

INTRODUCTION

Ryan Eras

One of the fundamental distinctions made in Scripture is between God the Creator, and man the creature. This is spelled out for us very early in the biblical record: "God created man in His own image, in the image of God He created him; male and female He created them" (Gen. 1:27). When we acknowledge God as Creator and two models of 'man' – male and female – created in His image, we are presented with the inescapable conclusion that our sexuality is part of the Creator's design plan, and central, in a very literal sense, to who we are.

When something, like sexuality, is common to all conscious human experience, there will be a corresponding abundance of ideas, beliefs, and assumptions about that thing. As Christians who take the authority of the Bible seriously, we should not be surprised to observe that Scripture has a good deal to say, both prescriptively and descriptively, about human sexuality and all its related subjects – marriage, children, masculinity, femininity, rules for lawful and unlawful sexual relationships, and much more.

A necessary reality of having many competing sets of ideas on sexuality is that many of those ideas are wrong. As Richard Weaver famously observed, ideas have consequences. Jeffery Ventrella, whose work is represented in this volume, extends Weaver's dictum to further assert that bad ideas have *victims*. The truth of this statement is on stark display in the realm of sexuality: consider the murderous culture of abortion, the mutilated bodies of 'transitioning' people, rape, divorce, and prostitution as just a few obvious examples. Our ideas about sex have real-life consequences for ourselves and others.

This short collection of essays from Ezra Institute staff and Fellows is offered as an introduction to some important aspects of sexuality. The title, Covenant Sexuality, is meant to acknowledge our dependent status on God as not only Creator, but as the personal and relational God who has established laws and norms in nature and in Scripture for human creatures who He made in His own image. This covenantal relationship places requirements on our thought and action in the realm of sexuality. As the apostle Paul exhorts us, "do you not know that your body is a sanctuary of the Holy Spirit who is in you, whom you have from God, and that you are not your own? For you were bought with a price: therefore glorify God in your body" (1 Cor. 6:19-20).

The subjects covered here are not presented as exhaustive. Some are perennial issues (pornography, family structure), some are lessons from a distinct period in history (the Puritan view of marriage), and others are profoundly, if not uniquely, twenty-first century phenomena (LGBTQ identities, preferred pronouns, and trans ideologies). Our hope is that you find these essays beneficial in bringing the clarity of Scripture and a Christian worldview to the storm of rhetoric and emotion on the one hand, or cold aloofness on the other, that often swirls around any discussion of sex.

SLAYING THE DRAGON OF OUR AGE:
PORNOGRAPHY AND THE THREAT
TO HUMAN NATURE
Nate Wright

For Christians who have studied their Bible and paid some attention to church history, it should come as no surprise that the unfolding story that God is telling throughout human history is a story with dragons in it. Dragons that must be slain. Enemies that must be put underneath the feet of Jesus in victory.

I've never seen a flesh and blood fire-breathing dragon, but their longstanding reputation as the embodiment of wrath, gluttony, sloth, greed, and a host of other vices communicates a profound spiritual truth about man, and the nature of evil and sin: sin is often enticing; the danger is part of the exhilaration, but it is an evil that is not just powerful, but actively and personally seeking to destroy you. This is attested to in Scripture as well:

> "If you do well, will not your countenance be lifted up? And if you do not do well, sin is crouching at the door; and its desire is for you, but you must master it." (Gen.

4:7)

"But each one is tempted when he is carried away and enticed by his own lust. Then when lust has conceived, it gives birth to sin; and when sin is accomplished, it brings forth death." (James 1:14-15

With this understanding, it should also come as no surprise that one of the most sinister dragons attacking our culture, our churches and our families is pornography. Never in history has sexual deviancy been so easy to access and so readily available even to young adolescents.

The negative influence of pornography and its addictive nature on the body, mind, and soul is well-documented,[1] not to mention the exploitation and enslavement of many men, women, and children who participate in the "industry."[2] This is reason enough for us to abominate pornography. And while the pervasiveness of this particular sin and the destruction it leads to is likely very familiar to many readers, I believe that we would be helped in understanding the foundation of this scorching, malevolent attack: pornography, ultimately, is an attack on the marriage bed and the dominion mandate that lies at the foundation of Christian purpose.

---

1   Kalivas, PW. "The neural basis of addiction: a pathology of motivation and choice." *American Journal of Psychiatry*, 2005; 162(8):1403.

2   ARPA Canada, "Policy Report for Parliamentarians," 2017, https://arpacanada.ca/wp-content/uploads/2016/03/ARPA-PolicyReport-Pornography-online2.pdf

In Genesis 1 we are told: Then God said, *"Let us make man in our image, after our likeness. And let them have dominion over the fish of the sea and over the birds of the heavens and over the livestock and over all the earth and over every creeping thing that creeps on the earth." So God created man in his own image, in the image of God he created him; male and female he created them. And God blessed them. And God said to them, "**Be fruitful and multiply and fill the earth and subdue it, and have dominion** over the fish of the sea and over the birds of the heavens and over every living thing that moves on the earth."* (Gen. 1:26-28, emphasis added)

This mandate is reiterated to Noah in Genesis 9 after the flood and is implied by Jesus to his disciples in what we call the Great Commission of Matthew 28. God created the world. The world was an untamed wilderness and Adam and Eve were meant to bring God's order to bear on the world around them. He gave them the blueprint in the garden, there they saw what Gods rule looked like when applied to physical creation. But the garden was only a small portion of the created world; if God's image-bearers populated and ordered the rest of creation then truly God's glory would cover the earth as the waters cover the sea (Hab. 2:14). So mankind was created to fill and form the world according to what their heavenly Father had modelled to them.

The only way we can succeed in this mission is if man and woman come together in covenant relationship, bear children and raise them for the task of godly dominion. *Therefore sex is the mechanism by which dominion takes place.* Fruitful procreation brings forth image-bearers who multiply the productive power of mom and dad. This is designed by God and it reflects his purpose for creation. This is why Satan has always attacked marriage. His attack started in the garden, continued through the patriarchs, persisted with the kings of Israel, and over the centuries it has only intensified.

Pornography is one of the primary means by which Satan attacks marriage in our modern culture and it is a direct attack on the dominion engine at the heart of every marriage: the marriage bed.

It was God who blessed man with a sex drive, with testosterone which, if not mastered, can make men lustful, impetuous, violent savages. But when man's sex drive, which God called very good, is mastered by the Holy Spirit and that force is pointed in the direction of fruitful dominion then it creates family, security and civilization.

There are very few things that Satan fears more than spirit-empowered patriarchs spending their lives on fruitful, representative rulership of the earth. That's how dominion gets taken. That's how the kingdom of heaven comes to the earth and God's will gets done on earth as it is in heaven.

But pornography wastes the sex drive of men and the civilization-building benefits of testosterone on cheap lust. It reduces sexuality to mere sexual gratification. It makes sex individualistic and selfish, which is the opposite of its biblical intention. In scripture not only do we see the constant biblical assertion that sex is meant for fruitful multiplication as God fills up the earth with his image-bearers, but we see specific times when the waste of life is condemned by God.

One example that comes to mind is when Onan, son of Judah fails to fulfill his Levirate duty and give his deceased brother an heir. In Genesis 38 it says, *"But Onan knew that the offspring would not be his. So whenever he went in to his brother's wife he would waste the semen on the ground, so as not to give offspring to his brother. And what he did was wicked in the sight of the Lord"* (Gen. 38:9-10).

Despite all the complex relationships that God gave to mankind, it is only to one relationship that He gave the good gift of sex. According to God's Word sexual expression is only permissible in a relationship between a man and a woman bound together in covenant love. To that union God gives the gift of sex, which serves the purpose of pleasure and fruitfulness.

Scripturally speaking pleasure is meant to be communal. God is triune, the fellowship within the Godhead is perfect and joyful, this is why when God made man, who is not three in one as God is, he said it is not good for man to be alone (Gen. 2:18). Adam was in relationship with God, but he needed companionship that was physical and that completed the triunity reflected in his creator. So God created woman, Eve, because human beings are communal creatures. Pornography reduces what is meant to be communal and plural to something individually gratifying.

Further, pornography completely ignores the fruitful direction of sexual pleasure. The one flesh union between a man and woman is meant to bring forth new life. In Ephesians 5 Paul says that he is sharing a profound mystery about the one flesh union between a husband and wife, about marital sex, that it reflects Christ and the church

(Eph. 5:32).

This mystery is speaking of the indwelling of the Spirit of God in the life of every believer. The fact that in marriage a man goes into a woman and the two become one is a physical picture of the Holy Spirit entering into every believer and empowering them to live lives of obedience and potency (Rom. 8:11). This explains the significance of sexual intimacy in marriage, but it also explains why Satan hates sex and why he has spent so much time attacking it through pornography. Christ in us, the hope of glory (Col. 1:27) is inextricably linked to Satan's demise. It is through his spirit-empowered church that God will crush His foe (Rom. 16:20). Because of this, Satan hates the reality of the indwelling Spirit, but he can do nothing to reverse it. All he can do is attack the physical representation, like a peasant too powerless to attack the King burns him in effigy, Satan strikes at the image.

As always, however, when Satan attacks he is not creative. Satan does not have the power to create; God alone is Creator, Satan is a usurper and a perverter. His attack relies on his ability to twist what God has already made, directing it or utilizing it for something other than what God intended. Satan cannot alter what something is, not even so-called evolution can do that, God's world is fixed. What Satan must do then is to make God's design for the thing he has created seem restrictive, boring or oppressive.

One of the functional benefits of frequent, satisfying sexual union in marriage is that it actually endows men and women with the tools necessary to carry out their calling as image-bearers. Much like the Spirit dwelling in the believer endows the Christian with the gifts, motivations and fruit of the spirit necessary to walk in obedience, sex cultivates masculinity and femininity. When a husband is engaged in sex he is physically hard, he enters, he takes initiative and he leads. When a woman is engaged in sex she is soft, she receives, she helps and she is led. These physical realities, when practiced frequently, create physical habits that are unique to men and women. It helps men be more like men and women be more like women.

Further to this the physical chemicals released, which are different in men and women during sex, actually reinforce qualities the Bible attributes differently to men and women. Men become more assertive, more confident and more protective. Women become more submissive, more content and more secure.

Pornography breaks down these sexual distinctions, it makes the act of sex androgynous and inward-focused, and it cultivates attributes of selfishness, impatience and anxiety. In short, pornography robs us not only of the uniqueness of our masculine and feminine qualities, but ultimately, in doing so, attacks our very ability to carry out the command given to mankind in the garden: to take godly dominion of the world.

When it comes to pornography, it is not an overstatement to say that the world hangs in the balance. Pornography threatens to disqualify and enfeeble Christians and render us incapable of carrying out our God-given purpose. If we cannot slay this dragon, it threatens to set the world on fire.

So, how do we slay this dragon?

Though much has been written on the topic of overcoming lust and pornography I believe the ancient Greeks powerfully expressed the true nature of lust.

In Greek mythology the sirens were humanlike creatures with alluring voices and devious motives. They were sometimes depicted as half-fish half-woman (mermaids) but more often described as more birdlike women who had the ability to sing songs of such allure and beauty that they would drive men mad who heard them.

Throughout the Greek epics there is an island called the Island of Sirens, a treacherous place where these beautiful creatures lived. The sirens would use their haunting melodies to lure ships and sailors toward their island. These sailors, following the music, would shipwreck on the reef and be consumed by the cannibalistic creatures. Most Greek heroes would avoid the island altogether even if it made their journey longer.

In Homer's famous *Odyssey* the protagonist, Odysseus, desiring to expedite his journey home to his wife Penelope, decides to pass the island. Odysseus' strategy to keep himself and his men safe was to have his sailors place beeswax in their ears to drown out the alluring sound of the sirens. Desiring to hear the legendary music however, Odysseus instructs his men to bind him tightly to the mast while they pass. He gives them strict instructions that no matter how mad he becomes, no matter how much he pleads, not to untie him.

The ship comes within range and the song of the sirens fills Odysseus' ears, driving him into a lustful craze. He strains against the bonds which keep him strapped to the mast. He longs to jump into the ocean and swim to the island, even though he knows it would mean his own death. Bewitched and under the tempting spell of the sirens' alluring song Odysseus is incapable of rational thought or self-control.

Once the ship passes and the songs fade to an echo Odysseus' sanity returns and he thanks his crew for following his orders and saving his life.

Most Christians attempt to slay the dragon of pornography in similar fashion. They seek accountability and physical restraint. They take data off their phone. They put their computer in a common room of the house. They install accountability software. These are all noble things and for those caught in the lair of this dragon I recommend them all. Plot against yourself, make it impossible, even when you are bewitched by the siren's song, to act upon your irrational lust.

But there is a better way.

Another Greek hero named Jason also encountered the sirens. He and the Argonauts had to sail past the island, but he employed a much better strategy for keeping his men safe. Jason brought Orpheus with him on his journey, who was said to be the greatest musician Greece had ever known; according to legend he was blessed by the gods to be able to play any instrument perfectly and had a voice so beautiful it could tame animals.

When the ship came within earshot of the entrancing song of the sirens Jason ordered Orpheus to the bow of the ship where he played a more beautiful song. The Argonauts were not bewitched in the same way Odysseus was because they were enjoying a song far more alluring.

This principle is not limited to Greek mythology. C.S. Lewis once called such things "True Myths:" stories that tell the truth about God's world, not because their authors were Christians but because our great Storyteller has embedded his truth into the fabric of the universe. *"Finally, brothers, whatever is true, whatever is honorable, whatever is just, whatever is pure, whatever is lovely, whatever is commendable, if there is any excellence, if there is anything worthy of praise, think about these things."* (Phil. 4:8) Paul is teaching the same principle, exhorting the Philippian church that they are to exercise dominion over their own minds. Paul tells them that one of the ways they win the battle against sin is by laying before their minds things that are beautiful and lovely.

When it comes to slaying the dragon of pornography we must begin by catching a better vision. We must become enraptured with a more beautiful song.

Christians who allow pornography to steal their strength and shipwreck their purpose lose their unique masculinity and femininity. They lose their ability to take godly dominion. They spill their seed and waste their time all for momentary gratification. In doing so they give up the beautiful vision of fruitful representative rulership. They give up the task of godly dominion. They disqualify themselves from playing a part in the unfolding drama of filling the earth with the glory of God as the waters cover the sea (Hab. 2:14). Do not be one of the warriors slain that Solomon warns his sons of in Proverbs 7:

24 And now, O sons, listen to me,
   and be attentive to the words of my mouth.

25 Let not your heart turn aside to her ways;
   do not stray into her paths,

26 for many a victim has she laid low,
   and all her slain are a mighty throng.

27 Her house is the way to Sheol,
   going down to the chambers of death.

RECLAIMING THE RAINBOW
RESPONDING TO THE LGBT CHALLENGES WITH GRACE & TRUTH
T.K. Fenske, MD, FRCPC, FCCP, FACC

Although secularized over the years to signify dreamy pot-o-gold optimism or new beginnings *somewhere over the rainbow*, it wasn't until the San Francisco Gay Freedom Day Parade celebration in 1978 that the rainbow symbol was co-opted by the non-heterosexual lobby group. In 1994, commemorating the 25th anniversary of the Greenwich Village Stonewall riots of 1969, the rainbow flag was internationally established as the symbol for the lesbian, gay, bisexual, and transgender (LGBT) cultural movement. As the abbreviation has expanded to 2SLGBTQi (adding the 2S aboriginal *two-spirited* to the beginning of the older contraction, and Qi denoting *queer* and *intersex* at the end), so too, has the spread of the rainbow. These days, rainbow flags seem ubiquitous, flying not just at gay rallies, or during *Pride summer*, but all year round and in all places, including schools, public libraries, businesses, and even draped over the chancels of some liberalized churches. Reminiscent of National Socialism in Germany with the widespread parading of swastika flags in the public square (churches included), the *Pride Flag* invasion is nothing less than a foisting of an ideology diametrically opposed to the Creator of the universe and his covenantal promises. It's a distorted rainbow revolution, pridefully boasting of what God condemns.

A Christian response to our culture's embrace of all things LGBT is rife with challenges, both on the political front, as we attempt to winsomely defend biblical truth in the public sphere, and on the home front, as we walk alongside and attempt to provide gentle counsel to those struggling with their sexual identity in our personal circle. The LGBT movement has targeted Christianity and is intentionally and systematically deconstructing family, marriage, parenthood, and gender. It's a daunting opposition to face, particularly since it demands not only passive *tolerance*, but complete and active *acceptance* and even *celebration*.

And these demands aren't merely idle threats. With the passing of the so-called *Conversion Therapy* Bill C-4,[1] there is in Canada a present risk of imprisonment for those who are deemed to have 'offended.' From faithful corporate preaching of the Word, to compassionate counsel, and even private family discussions, Bill C-4 is poised to criminalize Christian communication, including the Great Commission's call to gospel witness. With this bill, LGBT activists have effectively silenced concerned opposition, and as a result, threaten to rescind our hard-won freedom of speech. The ambition of this series of essays is to discuss these challenges, and provide an approach to how we might effective-

---

1   "Bill C-4: An Act to amend the Criminal Code (conversion therapy)," *Government of Canada*, last modified December 8, 2021, https://www.justice.gc.ca/eng/csj-sjc/pl/charter-charte/c4_1.html.

ly communicate our concerns to a growing anti-Christian culture. My hope is to provide the necessary equipping for the Christian community to not only meet this formidable challenge, but to recognize in the process opportunities for gospel witness and favor.

The LGBT movement represents the logical outworking of the *me-focussed* sexual revolution of 1960s, and parallels the rise in demand for personal autonomy – to be a law unto ourselves and "be as God" (Gen 3:5). At its core, the movement is grounded on an anti-Christian worldview, steeped in pagan ideology, with roots in the fertility cults of antiquity. Like the tip of an iceberg, the immoral sexual behaviors promoted by LGBT activists represent the visible surface-level aspects of a much larger underlying worldview, which directly challenges the biblical sexual ethic. The celebration of non-heterosexual expression is in line with Plato's *Symposium*, where the love of a man for a woman is considered the base and "lower form of love," whereas the love of a man for a man a "heavenly and higher love."[2] Such ideas have consequences, which permeate every aspect of culture, including the social, political, medical, psychological, moral, and spiritual landscape of our society. As explained by Dr. Peter Jones in his book *Whose Rainbow?* the decline in Christianity and rise in personal autonomy necessarily produces paganism. He comments, "Homosexuality is presented as part of a blossoming Western defence of civil and human rights and as an essential and beneficial building block of a progressive moral agenda…, but it is

---

2   Plato, *The Symposium*, trans. Christopher Gill (London: Penguin Classics, 2003).

not civil rights. It is the abandonment of theism in the last two generations of Western history, and the embrace of the spirituality of Eastern paganism."[3]

LGBT Narrative

In contrast to the creative, covenantal, sacrificial and sacred characteristics of biblical sexuality, the pagan worldview of the LBGT movement promotes the opposite. The LGBT narrative rejects the Bible and celebrates the very antithesis of the Christian sexual ethic. Central to this celebration is the emphatic non-binary pronouncement of sexuality. Instead of the sacred male and female distinction, there is a blurring of all boundaries, epitomized by androgyny, where male and female reduce down to a neither-nor neutral, sexually undefined person. Since this ideology flies in the face of reality, indoctrination needs to begin early and be propped up by repeated reinforcement. This is why pre-schoolers are read LGBT children's literature by drag queens in our public libraries, and why school children are daily encouraged to pick their own pronouns, play for either the boys' or girls' sports team, use either the male or female washroom, and choose whichever changeroom they prefer.[4] Otherwise, it's feared, children wouldn't give their gender or sexuality a second thought and simply be content with their God-given design, girls playing with dolls and skipping rope

3   Peter Jones, *Whose Rainbow? God's Gift of Sexuality: A Divine Calling* (Grimsby, ON: Ezra Press, 2020).

4   "Guidelines for best practices: creating learning environments that respect diverse sexual orientations, gender identities and gender expressions, *Government of Alberta*, last modified January 1, 2016, https://open.alberta.ca/dataset/9781460126240.

and boys playing with sticks and skipping rocks.

With loss of male/female distinction comes loss of function. Same-sex couples can't biologically reproduce, and mutilated, transgendered genitalia will never function in that elegant and complex capacity, either. Since having babies is no longer possible, this central role of our sexuality gets discarded. Rather than seen as a means of *procreation*, sex is strictly considered a form of *recreation*. As journalist Gregory Herdt observed, "only by disengaging sexuality from the traditions of family, reproduction, and parenthood was the evolution of the gay movement a social and historical likelihood."[5] Separated from God's design of male and female, sex is disengaged from family structure, and no longer functions for reproduction and child-rearing, but merely hedonistic pleasure. Instead of being protected within a covenantal relationship, sex is let loose and considered an impersonal act, even a commodity, where masturbation and the use of pornography are legitimized and encouraged. Rather than one-flesh covenantal fidelity, promiscuity is celebrated. Children are provided graphic material on sexual practices, positions, and products, and told "not to knock it till you try it."[6] Instead of *self-giving*, sex is all about *self-gratification*. No longer a means of tangibly expressing one's love for one's spouse, sex becomes an end in itself, and an idol. Deposing purity, honor and sacredness, sex becomes dirty, profane and perverse; men with other men,

5   *Homosexuality/heterosexuality: Concepts of sexual orientation.* McWhirter, Sanders and Reinisch, eds., Oxford University Press, © 1996.

6   *Alberta Teachers' Association*, last modified February 16, 2024, https://teachers-ab.libguides.com/lgbtq/general.

women with women, mixing and matching of multiple partners and orgies, with no taboos or limits, joining what God has separated, and separating what God has joined.

IMPOVERISHED CHURCH RESPONSE

As disturbing as this flagrant abuse of God's good gift of sex is to consider, what's even more troubling are the disappointing ways in which the church has responded to the LGBT movement. Instead of fulfilling its God-ordained role "to proclaim the gospel, observe the ordinances, and make disciples,"[7] winsomely serving as a counterpoint and corrective for societal transgressions, the church in our day has more often than not missed the mark. Some churches have chosen to simply condemn non-heterosexuality – no dialog, no engagement, no nothing, end of discussion. Others, in an attempt to avoid conflict, have tried to keep a neutral ground and remain silent on the issue, hoping it might just go away. Still others, trying to extend grace in some sort of misdirected way, have chosen to affirm the gender identity confusion of those who struggle with their sexuality, and have even resorted to raising the rainbow flag and joining in on Pride celebrations.

Although the hostile anti-Christian attacks lobbed by LBGT lobby groups can be vicious, our response to them shouldn't be. We have to guard ourselves from trying to fight fire with fire. Profanity and pettiness should have no place in our vocabularies. Rather, we need to exhibit the fruit of the Spirit, which is first patient and kind, gentle

7　*The London Baptist Confession of Faith of 1689.* https://www.chapellibrary.org/pdf

and self-controlled (Gal. 5:22-23). As Paul reminds us, "For though we live in the world, we do not wage war as the world does. The weapons we fight with are not the weapons of the world" (2 Cor. 10:3-4). This necessitates, regardless of how our opposition may choose to operate, that we restrict ourselves to the high road. William Ralph Inge observed that "The enemies of freedom do not argue; they shout and they shoot." However, our means to advance the Kingdom of God can't be accomplished with hostile protests or petty argumentation. It's important that we remain biblically faithful and ensure that our methods reflect our gospel message. Otherwise, we misrepresent Christ to the world, and only end up adding fuel to the leftists' fire in their branding of all Christians as "haters" and "bigots."

The attempt of the church to be neutral and avoid the LGBT controversies has been regarded as a thoughtful and gracious approach. In an interview on HuffPost, former President Jimmy Carter tried to argue that since "Jesus never said a word about homosexuality," we shouldn't either, particularly a harsh or condemning word.[8] As a skilled statesman and peacemaker, this long-lived politician shone like few others, but as an expositor of Scripture trying to handle the word of God, he shows his limitations. While the red letters of Jesus didn't include the word "homosexuality" per se, Jesus had plenty to say about condemning sexual immorality, and significantly raised the bar of sexual purity,

---

8   "President Jimmy Carter Authors New Bible Book, Answers Hard Biblical Questions," *HuffPost*, last modified March 19, 2012,
https://www.huffpost.com/entry/president-jimmy-carter-bible-book_n_1349570

pronouncing that "anyone who looks at a woman lustfully has already committed adultery with her in his heart" (Matt. 5:28). The Bible, taken as a whole, represents the authoritative Word of God with the voice of Jesus throughout; it places homosexuality clearly under the banner of sexual immorality, and condemns it explicitly (Lev. 18:22; 20:13; Rom. 1:26; 1 Cor. 6:9; 1 Tim. 1:9-10). While such proof texts shouldn't be used to clobber people, ignorance of God's word needs to be countered.

As the Christian influence on our culture has waned, so too, has the understanding of Scripture. Biblical illiteracy has become the norm in our society and even churches, and with it, many Christian churches suffer from doctrinal confusion and have become prone to liberal trends, such as actually believing the societal lie that "homophobia is the problem, not homosexuality," or the slogan "love is love." Slogans make for impoverished thinking. *Love* as some ill-defined passion may, indeed, equate with itself, but it isn't necessarily *good*. After all, someone could love to cheat, to steal, to use pornography… Only God is good and only the biblical definition of love – that "while we were yet sinners, Christ died for us" (Rom. 5:8) – should be our guiding principle for the concern for others.

While the silent treatment some churches give to these challenges may derive from a superficial treatment of Scripture, or possibly even represent an ignorance as to our fundamental calling to be salt and light in the world (Matt. 5:13-6) – to preserve what's godly and expose what's not – more likely, however, their "no comment" represents plain old cowardice, and betrays a fear of man. No one wants to offend others or be seen as harsh, but as the Bible makes clear, "The fear of man lays a snare, but whoever trusts in the Lord is safe" (Prov. 29:25). When we allow the fear of man to dominate our concerns, instead of the fear of the Lord, we are no longer trusting in God or believing that He reigns sovereign. Using our own wits and wisdom as a moral guide, we enter into tiger country, leaving ourselves wide open to temptation, compromise, and eternal destruction. Jesus warned *not to fear man*, but to *fear God*, "who can destroy both soul and body in hell" (Matt. 10:28).

And make no mistake, although trying to dance around LGBT controversy might provide some temporary side-stepping of conflict and maintenance of our charitable status-quo, in the end, this anemic approach will prove futile. LGBT activism is on the forward move. Just as the gay rights activists in Canada weren't satisfied merely with Pierre Trudeau's concession to decriminalize sodomy in 1969, so too, the LGBT activists won't be satisfied with our present state of non-heterosexual affirmation and Pride celebration. They won't stop until all obstacles have been completely removed from their steady forward advance into sexual depravity. The political sphere has already caved to their present demands, as has law, healthcare, arts and entertainment, media, business, and education. The church of Christ represents the final remaining bastion of truth and decency, and they've got us in their sights. As gay columnist Paul Varnell summarized, "The chief opposition to gay equality is religious. We may conduct our liberation efforts in the political sphere and even the cultural sphere, but always undergirding those and slowing our progress is the moral religious sphere. If we could hasten the pace of change there, our overall progress would accelerate – in fact, it would be assured."[9] And assured it has become, in part, thanks to the silent church.

The response of some churches to affirm and celebrate the LGBT movement has led to a fundamental compromise of the gospel of Christ. Proponents maintain that the Bible is fallible, that it represents a book of its time, and that it isn't particularly clear on the moral status of homosexuality. They assert the ancient sexual ethic of the Christian church is "irrelevant and offends moderns too much to be useful." They hold that because the Bible was misused in the past to justify slavery and anti-Semitism, it can't be regarded as a societal standard for contemporary human sexuality. Pastor Brian McLaren of the so-called *Emerging Church* stated, for example, that the beliefs of traditional evangelicals represent a "reactive, combative brand of religious fundamentalism that preoccupies itself with sexuality" and that "evangelicals who consider homosexuals sinners are really just looking for an enemy – a scapegoat."[10] A flagrant example of gospel compromise would be the recent promotion of the so-called *Sparkle Creed* by a liberal Lutheran church.[11] This heretical

9   Dallas, Joe. *The Complete Guide to Understanding Homosexuality: a Biblical and Compassionate Response to Same-Sex Attraction.* Harvest House Publishers ©2010. page 462.

10   Denny Burk, "Why Evangelicals Should Ignore Brian McLaren: How the New Testament Requires Evangelicals to Render a Judgment on the Moral Status of Homosexuality," *Themelios*, vol. 35, iss. 2, https://www.thegospelcoalition.org/themelios/article/why-evangelicals-should-ignore-brian-mclaren-how-the-new-testament-requires/

11   Joshua Arnold, "Progressive 'Christians' Can Now Confess

mockery of the Apostle's Creed refers to God to as "non-binary," Jesus as having "two dads," and the Holy Spirit as the "rainbow spirit" with the proclamation that "love is love is love, so beloved let us love."

THE GAY GOSPEL

In an attempt to reconcile pagan sexuality with the Christian worldview, gay advocates reinterpret Scripture to align with their autonomous desires. Treating the Bible as if it were a wax nose to be shaped any which way, they render homosexuality as simply another expression of God's diversity in the created order to be celebrated. In their "fresh understanding of the Bible," they propose that the sin of Sodom, for example (Gen. 19), wasn't in regards to homosexuality at all, but was about rape, inhospitality, or general wickedness, and the homosexuality cited in Leviticus 18:22 and 20:13 referred to prostitution or an idolatrous form of homosexuality.

These proponents of the Gay Gospel suggest that when Jesus healed the centurion's servant (who they suggest was "highly valued" because he was the soldier's gay lover), that Jesus gave tacit approval of homosexuality. So, too, they consider the comments Jesus made about eunuchs (Matt. 19:12) a favorable view of homosexuality, even though, of course, castration and sexual orientation are not at all the same. They go on to claim that the apostle Paul's comment about "men abandoning natural relations" (Rom. 1:26) was

Heresy with 'Sparkle Creed,'" *Washington Stand*, last modified June 29, 2023, https://washingtonstand.com/commentary/progressive-christians-can-now-confess-heresy-with-sparkle-creed.

in reference to *heterosexuals* who practice homosexuality, not born-that-way *genuine* homosexuals doing so. Their mistreatment of Scripture is a shameful attack on the integrity, sufficiency and authority of the Bible.[12] In essence, "they are turning to a different gospel – which is really no gospel at all... and are throwing people into confusion and trying to pervert the gospel of Christ" (Gal. 1:6-7). Not surprisingly, their twisted and tortured exegesis has no credible scholarly support.[13]

The fruit of the Gay Gospel has been bitter. This watering down and distortion of the gospel has proven to be detrimental for the liberalized churches, dividing leadership, splitting congregations, impairing gospel witness, invalidating missional outreach, and decimating membership and church attendance. Homosexuality is a critical watershed issue of our time. By endorsing the LGBT movement, the church has accelerated its own steady and swift decline in the West.[14] Leading this decline has been the United Church of Canada (UCC), which ordained openly gay clergy as early as 1992. Over the decade prior to the 2005 legalization of same-sex marriage in Canada, the UCC provided liturgical covenants for same-sex couples, and then in 2012, elected an openly gay moderator. Once the largest Protestant denomination in the country, the UCC is now but a dying remnant, forced to sell off its church real estate

12   Gilson, R. *Born Again This Way.* The Good Book Company © 2020.

13   Dallas, Joe. *The Gay Gospel: How Pro-Gay Advocates Misread the Bible*, Harvest House © 2007.

14   Jones, P. *The God of Sex: How Spirituality Defines your Sexuality.* Escondido, CA: Main Entry Editions ©2006.

in order to desperately keep afloat. Shrinking faster than any other denomination, the UCC lost over 40 percent of its affiliates in the past decade, with nationwide attendance declining to under 120,000 people, most of whom are elderly with no desire or means to move on.[15] The Anglican church of Canada has followed suit, both in their allegiance to the LGBT narrative, and with their resultant steep decline in parishioner base.[16] So too, the Lutheran Church in North America is also on the steep decline.[17] With the recent decision to bless same-sex couples, the Church of England likely isn't very far behind this decline, either. And why should it be otherwise? As Greg Bahnsen wisely said, "When the church begins to look and act like society, there is no reason for its continued existence."[18]

RESPONDING WITH GRACE AND TRUTH

As followers of Jesus, our response to the LGBT challenges needs to be one of grace and truth. It's critical that we

---

15   Julie McGonegal, "The United Church's numbers have dropped more than any other denomination," *Broadview*, last modified May 9, 2023, https://broadview.org/inside-united-church-decline/

16   Sean Frankling, "Anglican Church of Canada membership fell 10% each year in 2020 and 2021, data show," *Episcopal News Service*, last modified December 14, 2022, https://www.episcopalnewsservice.org/2022/12/14/anglican-church-of-canada-membership-fell-10-each-year-in-2020-and-2021-data-show/

17   Mathew Block, "Decline and Growth: A Look at the Lutheran World Today," *The Canadian Lutheran*, last modified February 28, 2022, https://www.canadianlutheran.ca/decline-and-growth-a-look-at-the-lutheran-world-today/

18   Bahnsen, G. L. *Always Ready: Directions for Defending the Faith*. American Vision and Covenant Media. ©1996.

maintain the tension between the exclusive truth claims of Christ and the inclusive grace of Christ. Although far easier to do only one or the other – either hold hard to the letter of Scriptural law and present a cold wall of opposition, or offer warm unqualified open-armed welcome – neither of these singular approaches are effective nor biblically faithful. It's not one or the other, but a measure of both, together. Jesus didn't dismiss the woman accused of adultery with disdain and disgust, saying "Go." Nor did he affirm her sexual behaviour and celebrate her lifestyle, saying "Go and sin." Rather, he protected her from harm and offered her abundant life free from the slavery of sin, saying, "Go and sin no more" (John 8:11). Therefore, our response to the LGBT challenges mustn't be one of cold condemnation, nor gushing affirmation.

Rather, without compromising the biblical sexual ethic, we need to respond winsomely, communicating both our *concern* for biblical truth and *care* for struggling individuals. "For the law was given through Moses; grace and truth came through Jesus Christ (John 1:17). If we capitulate on biblical truth, we forfeit the gospel and its redeeming power, and make ourselves complicit in the loss of a soul to eternal judgement; and if we fail to reach out in compassion and care, we miss the opportunity to witness and share the gospel's redeeming message. Analogous to an archer's bow, which is only useful under the tension of the bowstring (otherwise is but a weird bent stick, not even suitable for walking), as faithful followers of Christ, we need to hold fast to both biblical truth and winsome engagement in balanced tension. If we fail to do so, our efforts will yield little.

We'll either shut down dialog completely or get shut down ourselves, and run the risk of being compromised on one hand, or cancelled on the other. In either case, we'll join the sorry ranks of "those who do not turn to the most High, are like a bow gone slack" (Hosea 7:16).

It's also important to separate our response to the activist movement, on the one side, from our response to someone who is struggling with their sexuality, on the other. We need to realize that these are two very separate conversations, both set on the same foundation, but expressed with different language and means. I came to this realization when I had an intense exposure to the non-heterosexual community. It was in the mid-'80s during the height of the AIDS epidemic in Canada. I was a medical student at St. Paul's hospital in downtown Vancouver, and did my clerkship before the introduction of anti-retroviral therapy, when acquiring HIV was akin to being given a death sentence. During that same time, my father, who was a United Church minister, was faithfully preaching the full counsel of Scripture and actively pushing back against the encroaching gay gospel. Our frequent late-night conversations equipped me to easily recognize the worldview challenges posed by the gay movement, but did little to prepare me in my conversations with gay patients. That required the frontline experience which I acquired during those harrowing times.

As a student intern, I directly followed 8 to 10 patients at a time, the majority of whom were gay men about my age, dying of AIDS. It was heart-wrenching watching their opportunistic infections and cancers progress and, despite our best efforts, consume them. During this training time, while I was trying to memorize my differential diagnosis lists and develop my physical exam techniques, I witnessed the devastation of this pitiless disease on the human condition. All of my patients died, and I was often the one called by the nurses to pronounce them dead. It was a brutal boot camp for learning medicine, to be sure, but the experience gave me on-the-job training in humility and compassion, as I endeavored to respond to the suffering of my patients. As well, I had repeated opportunities to have long conversations, which went well beyond the surface medical management of their disease, and touched on their existential suffering. This is because as a student, I had a certain luxury of time, and I spent mine not just chasing down lab results and writing up histories, but at my patients' bedsides, talking with them, getting to know their families, their lovers, and meeting their extensive friend groups and community of support. I learned something of their struggles, their frustrations and brokenness, and their desperate desire for acceptance.

And as I spent time with them, listening to their stories, and developing a relationship with them, I was able to get past the initial facades, breaching topics of identity and faith. I shared my testimony with many of them, and at poignant moments, even prayed with some. Although I never agreed with their sexual confusion nor gay lifestyles, my heart broke for them nonetheless, and I have since felt drawn to reach out to LGBT patients with care and compassion.

Responding to the Struggling Individual

If we want to meaningfully engage those within the LGBT community and have constructive conversations with them, we need to be generous and communicate sentiments of concern. Opening our interactions with divisive comments about the causation of non-heterosexuality or arguments about the changeability of sexual orientation will unlikely be fruitful, and add more heat than light to the discussion. It's not us against them, after all; non-heterosexuals are not the enemy. Sexual brokenness comes from our sinful nature magnified by our sexualized culture. It's been estimated that over 1/3 of the Internet bandwidth is devoted to viewing pornography, which has infiltrated every part of our society, the church included.[19] We are all sexually broken to some extent, and if left to our own devices can easily fall into temptations of sinful sexual thoughts, even deeds. As the apostle Paul reminds us, "for all have sinned and fall short of the glory of God" (Rom 3:23). We are all in need of Christ's redemption and the ongoing sanctifying work of the Holy Spirit, and we won't completely escape the conundrum of sexual sin until heaven and earth are made new. So, we would do well to adopt a posture of humility, "quick to listen, slow to speak and slow to become angry" (Jas. 1:19). As we listen, we should do so not with the intent of winning an argument, but in order to make points of contact that will allow us to steer the conversation towards Jesus, the ultimate remedy. We need to endeavor to make Jesus the issue, not sexuality. As Mark Yarhouse wisely emphasizes

---

19 "Pornography Statistics," *Covenant Eyes*, last modified 2024, http://www.covenanteyes.com/pornstats/

about these difficult conversations, "the goal is not hetero-sexuality, but holiness."[20]

Gender confusion and the sinful behaviour that ensues are but symptoms of a far larger problem, namely, mis-placed identity. The prevailing messaging promoted by our LGBT-embracing culture is that same-sex attractions are natural, even God-given, and that such feelings not only in-dicate one's *true-you* core identity, but that sexual behaviour is the central means to fulfillment. This so-called *Gay script* conflates the three distinct elements of sexual attraction, sexual behaviour, and gay identity into an all-in-one pack-age. Even though these are each clearly distinct, if feelings are felt, it is suggested, behaviour and even permanent lifestyle adoption must inevitably follow.

Of course, this just isn't true. Feelings don't mandate behaviour. Just because some scantily-clad woman walking past me in the grocery store might transiently catch my attention, it doesn't mean that I, a married man, should follow her into the produce section to check out the toma-toes and get her phone number, nor that I should make a lifestyle of hanging out at the deli in the hopes of making bacon. A fleeting reflex feeling or thought doesn't necessitate an adulterous behavioural response, nor a swinger lifestyle. We are not victims of instinct, confined to a programmed script of behaviour, but have been created in God's im-age, and therefore have the freedom to choose our actions. Same-sex attraction represents temptations, not destiny. Like all other temptations, such as over-indulgence of alco-

20 Yarhouse, M. *Homosexuality and the Christian: A Guide for Parents, Pastors, and Friends.* Bethany House©2010.

hol, over-eating pastries, binging TV, or lining up for Sunday blow-out shopping extravaganzas, they can't be given a life of their own and remain unchecked. No matter how much like "thorns in the flesh" same-sex attractions may be, they don't need to result in homosexual behaviour, and certainly not a gay lifestyle. Those who hold up sexuality as ultimate are doomed to disappointment. It's not just Mick Jagger who can't get no satisfaction; no one can on those terms. No sexual experience – heterosexual or non-heterosexual – can live up to such dizzyingly high expectations, and identities formed around them won't be able to satisfy our fundamental needs as human beings.

By opposing God's design for sexuality, our culture has set into motion an unparalleled identity crisis, and at the same time, opened up a giant gospel opportunity for the Christian community to witness God's love to broken people. Our task, as followers of the risen Lord, is to provide an alternative script for those who struggle in sexual sin. We need to emphasize that it's not sex that's ultimate, but God, as revealed in the life, death, resurrection and calling of Jesus Christ. At its center, our identity is not a sexual issue at all, but a creational one that can only be truly defined by our Creator. While we are undeniably sexual beings, our *core* identity doesn't reside in our sexuality, but is contained within the eternal relationship of the Triune living God. By necessity, our *I am* must be grounded in the *Great I am*. When we fail to grasp this biblical reality, choosing instead something smaller or distorted, such as our perceived gender or preferred sexual behaviour, we generate within ourselves an unquenchable misdirected thirst for personal significance, social acceptance, and individual security.[21]

While the LGBT community attempts to provide these by affirming same-sex feelings, celebrating non-binary gender choices, and validating non-heterosexual relationships and gay lifestyle experiences, desperate emptiness remains. It's well-documented that the LGBT group, taken as a whole, is at a substantially higher risk for poor health outcomes as compared to the general population.[22] Not only do they suffer from higher rates of depression, but also substance addictions, eating disorders, post-traumatic stress disorder and sexual abuse, and they have a staggeringly high suicide rate. Despite the propagated narrative that all this stems from societal stigmatization, these tragic problems are seen to occur at the same rates in the most LGBT-affirming of countries, as well.[23]

It's imperative, then, that we communicate the need for an identity in Christ, and let those who label themselves under the LGBT umbrella know that they are image-bearers of God, fearfully and wonderfully made, and dearly loved by Him, the lover of their souls. Sharing our own personal testimony of faith is a powerful means to do so. As we tell of our own struggles with sin over the years and our own experiences with misplaced identity, such as with a work-based identity, a family-role-based identity, or a fitness-based identity, for example, we can forge points of contact, and begin "to make the teaching about God our Saviour attrac-

---

21   Anderson, Neil T. *Living Free in Christ* ©1993 Regal Books.

22   *The Fenway Guide to Lesbian, Gay, Bisexual & Transgender Health*, 2nd Edition.

23   Dhejne, C, et.al. Cohort Study in Sweden. 2011; 6(2).

tive" (Titus 2:10). Jesus was a single celibate male and lived the perfect life, completely obedient to the law of God and completely fulfilled in every way. He didn't come to earth for acceptance, significance, nor security, but to glorify God and to have mercy on sinners. With this in mind, we need to underscore that our core identity – including our essential needs for acceptance, significance, and security –be formed around a personal relationship with Christ, and Christ alone.

At the base of our engagement with members of the LGBT community must be our concern for not only their present wholeness, but their eternal hope of salvation. God has given us the biblical sexual ethic for both our present flourishing and to prepare us for eternal communion with Him in glory. This mandates that we don't just leave our conversations on the superficial plane of climate and Coke, but go deeper and address the essential matters of sin and salvation. Jesus was a friend to sinners, to be sure. However, he didn't leave them in their sins, but called all people to "repent and believe in the gospel" (Mark 1:15). If all our friendship with non-heterosexuals does is comfort them in their sins, we've done them a serious disservice, and not acted as a friend at all. Homosexual behaviour is sexual sin. And like other sexual sins, including adultery, heterosexual promiscuity, serial monogamy, premarital sex, and mastur-bation, it needs to be called out as a sin requiring confession and repentance.

Paul exhorts us to "flee from sexual immorality," em-phasizing that "all other sins a man commits are outside his body, but he who sins sexually sins against his own body,"

43

reminding us that we "were bought at a price... therefore honor God with your body" (1 Cor. 18-20). It doesn't matter if they claim they were "born that way." We are all born into a sinful nature inherited from our first parents and "must be *born again*" (John 3:3). This requires a 180-degree about-face turning away from our old *sinful identity* to embrace our new *true identity* in Christ. As Paul clarified, "if anyone is in Christ, he is a new creation. The old has passed away; behold, the new has come" (2 Cor. 5:17). A gay lifestyle, no matter if it's "monogamous and sincere," is still misdirected and sinful. The same applies to gay marriage...raising the thorny issue of what to do if one receives an invitation to a "gay marriage" celebration.

RESPONDING TO AN INVITATION
TO A GAY WEDDING

A wedding is not like a dinner invitation or a graduation open house or a retirement party. A Christian wedding is, first and foremost, a worship service from beginning to end, celebrating the holy union between one man and one woman with God at the centre. As God's first institution, marriage bookends the beginning of the Bible and the end; it represents the fundamental building block of human community, and has historically been the foundation of Western civilization.[24] Those present at the solemnization of matrimony are not just casual observers, but are witnesses who are granting their approval and support for the holy vows that are being made. Worship of God and celebration

---

24   Zimmerman, CC. *Family and Civilization*. Intercollegiate Studies Institute ©2008.

of a holy union cannot be done if God's Word is profaned. Since the gay union being celebrated can't be biblically sanctioned as an act of worship, our participation in the service lends credence to a lie. Out of obedience to Christ and because of the nature of the wedding event itself, we cannot in good conscience participate in a service of false worship, nor celebrate a union that shouldn't be celebrated.

This is true for secular gay weddings, as well. There's nothing in the secular nature of a wedding ceremony that makes it any less of a celebration of a union. When we attend such a wedding, we are publicly endorsing the gay union before a watching world. Although attending a non-Christian heterosexual wedding poses certain challenges for the Christian attendee in terms of the misdirection of the ceremony, at least God's design of husband and wife is still being upheld. As a result, we can hope and pray that the couple will in time be convicted by the Holy Spirit and come to a saving faith in Christ, and lead Christian lives as a couple. However, the same cannot be said for the homosexual couple. For non-heterosexuals, our prayer would be that they would come to a saving faith in Christ and leave their lives of sin, their gay relationships included.

If this all sounds "not very loving," we need to understand that genuine love means telling the truth, not condoning a lie. Just as we must not buy into the contemporary word games of using imaginary gender designations, nor conflicting pronouns, so too, we shouldn't fuel sexual sin by celebrating a gay union. This even holds true for Christian families with gay or transgendered children. We need to communicate our sincere love and concern for them and do our utmost to maintain our relationship with them, but we can't condone their sexual sin nor celebrate their sinful lifestyle or union. Besides, "loving across our differences" is a two-way street. We should take time to listen to the gay couple and hear why our attendance means so much to them, by all means; but to be fair, they also need to listen to us, and understand why our faith in Christ and obedience to the Bible mandate our declining to attend. In all of these considerations, we mustn't lose sight of the eternal wedding promised by Jesus, that we as the Church of Christ and His Bride, have been "invited to the marriage supper of the Lamb" (Rev. 19:19).

RESPONDING TO THE LGBT MOVEMENT

As we broaden our discussion to address the LGBT *movement* and consider the challenges it poses to our society, it's important that we continue to balance grace and truth in tension. We need to keep in mind that in the middle of the movement are broken people. We mustn't be the cold and callous frozen chosen. Rather, as we discuss this inflammatory topic, the first thing out of our mouths must be *concern* for those who are suffering in gender confusion and struggling in sexual sin. At the same time, we can't just be bleeding hearts and open doormats to every sort of doctrinal distortion and cultural denigration. We need to honor King Jesus, both in our words of compassion, as well as in our faithful witnessing to His revealed truth.

It's critical to realize what's at stake here, both on earth and in heaven. Sexuality *is* a gospel issue! The LGBT movement outright rejects the gospel of Christ and challenges the church's very identity, purpose, and view of the Word of God. This spirit of rebellion is doing harm to numerous vulnerable groups within our society, including our children, who are being indoctrinated into this pagan ideology and placed at risk for sexual exploitation. But there are also those within the LGBT community who have been abandoned and continue to struggle with gender dysphoria and same-sex attraction, and others who are left to deal with the aftermath of cross-sex hormonal manipulation therapy and its inherent havoc and side effects, or the horror of their gender-transitioned mutilation.[25] And most to be pitied are those who have transitioned to the opposite sex, and in the process, have come to realize their vast mistake, deeply regretting their decision. This de-transitioning group continues to experience levels of stigmatization from the heterosexual community, while simultaneously being shunned from the LGBT community, which accepts gender transition as a one-way street only.[26]

With the rejection of the biblical sexual ethic, society's floodgates have been opened for unbridled sexual depravity. Although slippery slope arguments for gay marriage were heavily criticized, we need only look back over the past fifty years since the removal of homosexuality from the DSM (Diagnostic and Statistics Manual) list of psychiatric disor-

25   Jaclyn M. White Hughto and Sari L. Reisner. Trans*gender Health* Vol. 1, No. 1 A Systematic Review of the Effects of Hormone Therapy on Psychological Functioning and Quality of Life in Transgender Individuals. Jan. 2006.

26   Vandenbussche, E. (2021) Detransition-Related Needs and Support: A Cross-Sectional Online Survey, *Journal of Homosexuality*, DOI: 10.1080/00918369.2021.1919479.

ders in 1973, to see the reality of those concerns [27] Unlike the wildly inaccurate COVID-19 pandemic predictions of population decimation or the exaggerated forecasting for global warming, the fears raised about where homosexuality might lead our society have proven prophetically accurate.[28] What once was unthinkable in private is now celebrated in public. This includes the embrace of sadism, masochism, exhibitionism and voyeurism, polygamy, conjoint marriage (union of three or more individuals) and polyamory (multiple simultaneous partners), with pedophilia, incest, zoophilia (sexual attraction to animals) and bestiality fast approaching.[29,30] No perverse sexual fetish, no matter how disturbing to our sensibilities, will remain taboo for much longer. Sin is progressive, and offence, as it gets repeated, tends to lessen over time.

Resistance is certainly required, and some is already occurring in various places in our society. This has included students participating in the National Pride Flag Walk-Out Day, pro-family rallies of Christians and Muslims joining together to protest against LGBT ideology in school curricula, and NHL players refusing to wear Pride jerseys during

27   Drescher, J. Out of DSM: Depathologizing Homosexuality. *Behav Sci* (Basel). 2015 Dec; 5(4): 565–575.

28   Bahnsen. GL. *Homosexuality: a Biblical View*, Baker Books © 1978.

29   Miller D. Sexual Depravity Continues to Expand. https://apologeticspress.org/sexual-depravity-continues-to-expand-2691/

30   Holoyda, BJ. Bestiality Law in the United States: Evolving Legislation with Scientific Limitations. *Animals* (Basel). 2022 Jun; 12(12): 1525.

games.[31] In addition, there have been successful boycotts against the clothing store, Target, the LA Dodgers baseball franchise, and Disney, as well as with Anheuser-Busch customers making their distaste known about the company's Pride marketing, by buying beer other than Bud Light.[32]

As a Christian community, though, our best form of pushback is through the faithful proclamation of the gospel and the unwavering commitment to educate our children in biblical truth. Never more than now, the church of Christ needs to be the church of Christ, welcoming all sinners, yet "unashamed of the gospel…the power of God for the salvation of everyone who believes" (Rom. 1:16). This means preaching the entire counsel of Scripture, emphasizing our creational reality and including the portions of Scripture considered "too inflammatory to read." Out of solidarity, many churches across North America have committed to annually preaching on the biblical sexual ethic in January as a way of marking the anniversary of the passing of "anti-conversion" Bill C-4, the Canadian legislation that equates biblical truth to myth and criminalizes Christian conversation. While this is well and good, such faithful preaching of the Word shouldn't be limited to but one day a year, but define the Christian pulpit year-round. There is risk here, but if the Church doesn't stand strong, how can we expect our surrounding society to do so?

31   https://www.campaignlifecoalition.com/MassiveResistance-toLGBTQPridesparked

32   Chloe Berger, "From Bud Light to Target, Pride month saw rainbow capitalism dim in 2023," *Fortune*, last modified June 30, 2023, https://fortune.com/2023/06/30/bud-light-target-rainbow-capitalism-dimmed-june-2023/

As for teaching our children, we would do well to heed the model provided in the Torah, to teach the words of Scripture "diligently to your children, and…talk of them when you sit in your house, and when you walk by the way, and when you lie down, and when you rise" (Deut. 6:7). Although I endorsed the public school system when my own boys were school-aged, twenty years ago, it has become increasingly difficult, if not impossible, for Christian parents to rationalize sending their children to public school today. I used to hold to the notion that vibrant family discussion around the dinner table could undo the school's indoctrination. While this may have been naïve in the past, such thinking today is plainly foolhardy and borders on irresponsible. With few exceptions, the anti-Christian agenda is rife and unrelenting in the public school system. This is even true for Roman Catholic schools, as evidenced by student Josh Alexander's suspension and serial arrests for protesting against biological males sharing school washrooms and changerooms with females.[33]

So, we need to not only defend our right to teach our own children, but we have to do it and do it well. And as we do, it's critical we don't aim to just shelter them from the LGBT onslaught, but prepare them to think Christianly and be able to engage the posed challenges wisely. We need to equip them to be soldiers of the cross for the dark and desperate times that lie ahead, and "always be prepared to give an answer to everyone who asks them to give the reason

33   "I Stand with Josh Alexander," *Liberty Coalition Canada*, last modified 2024, https://libertycoalitioncanada.com/i-stand-with-josh-alexander/

for the hope that they have...with gentleness and respect"
(1 Peter 3:15).

Answering Questions of Gender Diversity and Homosexual Causation

In our present confused era, questions of biological gender
diversity and non-heterosexual causation will need to be
addressed. Children are being taught that the sexual characteristics of biology, gender identity, gender expression, and
sexual attraction all operate on a spectrum, and that they
must define these terms for themselves. While advocating
certain ideologies can cause people's convictions to bend
with the breeze of the times, biology doesn't bend. There is
only male and female. Exceptions, while they exist, are rare
and serve to prove this immutable reality. Sexual developmental disorders, grouped together under the umbrella term
"intersex," are commonly highlighted to make an argument
for biological gender diversity. However, intersex conditions
represent developmental *disorders*, not examples of *normal*
biology. They occur if there is either a hormonal imbalance
or a genetic error, and are considered disorders because of
the resultant dysfunction. With increasing biological aber-
rancy comes a decrease in sexual function. As a result, the
vast majority of intersex individuals are unable to reproduce.

Examples include the hormonal disorder Congenital
Adrenal Hyperplasia (CAH) in which there is an over-pro-
duction of cortisol (which is converted to androgen) and
causes some degree of virilisation of female genitalia. As

well, Androgen Insensitivity Syndrome (testicular femini-
zation syndrome) is caused by non-functional testosterone
receptors. The endogenous testosterone is converted to
estrogen which causes the development of female secondary
sex characteristics, including female genitalia. Although
these patients are unable to menstruate, they are usually
raised as female and generally adopt a sexual orientation no
different than normal 46XX genotype females. Other rarer
forms of hormonal imbalance can give rise to hermaphro-
dism, in which there is a discrepancy between the external
and internal sexual and genital organs, sometimes resulting
in ambiguous genitalia. Examples of genetic anomalies
that cause sexual developmental disorders include Turner's
Syndrome, where females are missing an X chromosome
(46X_), and Klinefelter's Syndrome where males have an
extra X chromosome (47XXY), both of which are associated
with infertility. In any case, making an argument that intersex conditions represent examples of biological diversity
would be analogous to making the ridiculous assertion that
congenital heart defects, which produce cardiac inefficiency
in mild cases and fatality in severe, represent a spectrum
of normal cardiac morphologies. While there is, indeed, a
range of normality seen in medicine, it remains critical to
be able to differentiate normal function from dysfunction.
Intersex conditions are, by definition, disorders character-
ized by dysfunction.

In terms of non-heterosexual causation, the jury is still
out. Numerous studies have been undertaken over the years
to investigate this question, including biological studies
involving twins, molecular genetics, hormonal effects, and

brain structure. The findings indicated that if genetics do play a role, they require a certain social context for their expression, such as a less-gendered childhood socialization. As well, extensive environmental studies have been undertaken assessing correlation of adverse childhood experiences, social and cultural environments, and parental influences to sexual orientation. Most striking was the finding that non-heterosexuals are about two to three times more likely to have experienced childhood sexual abuse as compared to heterosexuals, suggesting that this is a significant contributing factor in many cases.[34]

However, taken together, multiple pathways seem to contribute to a particular person experiencing same-sex attractions and homosexual orientation, where no one path fits all. The claim that sexual orientation is an innate, biologically fixed property of human beings – the idea that people are "born that way" – is certainly *not* supported by scientific evidence.[35] In fact, longitudinal studies of adolescents suggest that, if anything, sexual orientation may be quite fluid over the lifespan of some people, with one study estimating that as many as 80% of males who report same-sex attractions as adolescents no longer do so as adults.[36]

---

34   Andrea L. Roberts, M. Maria Glymour, and Karestan C. Koenen, "Does Maltreatment in Childhood Affect Sexual Orientation in Adulthood?," *Archives of Sexual Behavior* 42, no. 2 (2013): 161 – 171, http://dx.doi.org/10.1007/s10508-012-0021-9.

35   Sexuality and Gender: Findings from the Biological, Psychological, and Social Sciences. *The New Atlantis* (Special Report) – Lawrence Mayer and Paul McHugh. August 2016 (http://www.thenewatlantis.com/publications/number-50-fall-2016).

36   Ritch C. Savin-Williams and Geoffrey L. Ream, "Prevalence

Lisa Diamond, lead researcher of the American Psychological Association (APA) and avowed lesbian activist, stated that "viewing sexuality as exclusively two types – heterosexual and homosexual – that are rigid and unchangeable no longer applies," and is telling LGBT activists to "stop promoting the myth."[37] There's a sad irony in play when we see people in the church promoting arguments that even LGBT activists are now rejecting.

In conclusion, the devil wants people to think that they're either too good for the gospel, eliminating the need for repentance, or too bad, undermining the need for faith. In this fallen world of sexual brokenness, none of us are 'straight' in a certain sense – "all, like sheep, have gone astray" (Isaiah 53:6) – and are in desperate need of salvation. Fortunately, God's promises stand and are available to all who are forgiven of sin by faith in Jesus Christ. The rainbow functions to both remind God of his covenant relationship with us, and to remind us of his great mercy, grace, and power. We mustn't forget that the rainbow belongs to God and not to LGBT activists. Our mandate, then, is to reclaim the promise of the rainbow, and be the church that God intended us to be. We need to see these present LGBT challenges as opportunities to witness God's saving love, and demonstrate care and compassion to those in need, leaning on the gospel message, so that human flourishing and abundant life might displace misery and devastation. Judgement and Stability of Sexual Orientation Components During Adolescence and Young Adulthood," *Archives of Sexual Behavior* 36, no. 3 (2007): 385 – 394, http://dx.doi.org/10.1007/s10508-006-9088-5.

37   Lisa M. Diamond, *Sexual Fluidity* (Cambridge, Mass.: Harvard University Press, 2008), 52.

is surely coming, but it won't be with water this time. So, we must implore those caught up in sexual sin to give their hearts to Jesus that they might be set free from the bondage of sin, and saved from God's wrath.

Who do You Say I Am?

Gender-affirming Pronouns
and the Image of God
Jeffery J. Ventrella

The pressure rises on campus, in the public square, and in the church: Use someone's "gender affirming" pronoun or else be deemed "offensive" at best, or a bigot at worst. And, in the Christian milieu, this is often seen as providing passport to affirm the trans-challenged individual or else risk permanently conceding a hypothetical subsequent "gospel conversation."

It's almost pitched as: "if you uptight Christians would only have the decency to use the preferred pronoun, then the gates of heaven would fly open without impediment." How ought we to navigate this quite real and increasingly prominent situation? Is the issue of pronoun usage merely a matter of niceness and interpersonal courtesy?

Let's begin with a thought experiment: If one calls his car "water" that is one thing. However, if he puts his "water" in his garage and closes the door, secure in his own supposed noetic autonomy that his "water" is in the garage, what happens upon re-opening the door? Will he be greeted by a puddle?

Of course not; calling or labeling a car "water" does not mean that it becomes liquid. This is to confuse the language label with the actual thing. Labeling a car "water" will not convert it to being a puddle.[1]

In the same way, there is in fact an underlying reality when it comes to sex and reproduction in humans – just as there is for all mammals and other higher species. Every cell in your body, every neuron in your brain, is either male in its genetic makeup (XY) or female (XX). Your body can produce eggs, or it can produce sperm. Neither words, hormones, nor scalpels can change these and many other objective and sex-linked facts about you that you did not choose, that were handed to you at the first instant that you became you – at the instant of conception.

N.T. Wright explains the central theological flaw committed by confusing a chosen label with actual reality:

We are not, after all, defined by whatever longings and aspirations come out of our hearts, despite the remarkable rhetoric of our times. In the area of human well-being, that is the road to radical instability; in the area of theological beliefs, it leads to Gnosticism (where you try to discern the hidden divine spark within yourself and then be true to it).[2]

Calling things whatever one desires is not a Christian

---

1 Illustration taken from British thinker and blogger, Dan Moody in 2016.

2 N.T. Wright, *The Day the Revolution Began*, (New York: HarperCollins, 2016), 398.

exercise; it is rather a Gnostic, and hence pagan exercise, leading to instability and stifling human flourishing. There's more to personal pronoun usage than courtesy and niceness.

Let's also consider language and its role and use in general. Language stems from the eternal Word (John 1:1), who is Truth (John 14:6), and who cannot lie (Num. 23:19).[3] Accordingly, language when used by humans, those created in the image and likeness of this God, should be used for conveying truth.

Yet, what about when engaging with unbelieving suffering souls struggling with (or embracing) "gender dysphoria"? Shouldn't using their preferred personal pronoun be seen as a tangible act of loving one's neighbor? Don't we risk "offending" or shutting down the conversation by tying the pronoun to the person's sex? How should we think about this at the retail level where real people matter?

Let's first be clear about what loving one's neighbour biblically entails. James K.A. Smith provides keen insight:

> If we truly love our neighbors, *we will bear witness* to the *fullness to which they are called. If we truly desire their welfare, we should proclaim the thickness of moral obligations that God commands as the gifts to channel us into flourishing, and labor in hope that these might become the laws of the land, though with appropriate levels of expectation.*[4]

3   For a comprehensive approach, consider Vern Sheridan Poythress, *In the Beginning was the Word: Language, A God-Centered Approach*, (Wheaton, IL; Crossway, 2009).

4   James K. A. Smith, *Awaiting the King: Reforming Public Theology* (Grand Rapids: Baker Academic, 2017), 163. Emphasis added.

So it is actually profoundly *unloving* to reinforce notions that detract from a person's flourishing, or which compromise the moral duty to which God calls them. We do no favours by mistakenly equating niceness with actual reality-based kindness and love.

And, let's remember that "loving neighbour" is penultimate, not ultimate. It's the *second* great commandment. The *first* also necessarily bears on this question, and that commandment demands that we first love God with our entire being, including our mind (Matt. 23:34-40). This means, among other things, that a God-defined thing must control a self-labeled thing. Because humans are creatures, we *receive*, that is, discern, not *determine*, the Creator's description and interpretation of reality, including ethical reality (cf. Heb. 5:14). Misnaming reality in the name of personal preference or desire fails to justify that misnaming. Moreover, affirming someone's error in this regard contributes to their culpable suppression of truth (Rom. 1:18-32); knowledge of the created reality of gender is something 'hardwired' into us by virtue of our being made in the image of God.

How does all this relate to interacting with a "gender confused" neighbour who insists on your using a pronoun that defies the real reality of his or her sex? Here are a few thoughts.

First, there is a difference between personal pronouns and names. Personal pronouns refer to real persons and thus invoke and reference creational norms associated with those real persons, that is, the metaphysical reality of those persons. Names, in contrast, are labels *applied* to metaphysical reality, not in essence reflecting that reality itself. In other words, at bottom, there are men and women, but not necessarily Bob or Toby or Sam. A woman who assumes her husband's surname as is customary in some cultures doesn't cease to be a woman, nor does her metaphysical status change when her name changes.

A single name, because it is a label, not a metaphysical reality, can refer to both sexes, whether male or female[5] and a person can possess multiple names. Think of the "alternative" names of Daniel and his friends in Babylonian captivity. They had multiple names, but only one sex. Or consider Saul aka Paul. *Names* are thus *assigned*, while *sex* simply *is*. No one is born with a name; they are born, however, with a determined and immutable sex. Personal pronouns necessarily refer to sex[6], unlike names, which may or may not do so. Gender ideology advocates recognize this truth, which is why they adamantly insist that others use preferred personal pronouns.

Second, and expanding on this reality, God created mankind with a set metaphysical, binary complementarity called "male and female" (Gen. 2; cf. Matt. 19). This is what mankind is in real reality, and no existential desire, personal preference, cosmetic camouflage, hormonal infusion, or tissue-destroying surgery alters – or can alter – that reality – these techniques can only distort it. Sex can be superficially

5   Recall that King David's wife, Saul's daughter, was named "Michal." (1 Sam. 18). Other contemporary examples include Pat, Shannon, Leslie, Fran, Robin, Ashley, et al.

6   Gender ideology advocates recognize this truth, which is why they adamantly insist that others use preferred personal pronouns.

obfuscated, it cannot be obliterated.

Third, Jesus teaches that the process of becoming holy
– sanctified – flows from applying a word-based truth
(John 17:17). If one instead employs a reality-denying
pronoun—calling a male "her" or "she" – one is thereby
withholding, obscuring, or obstructing the means by which
a confused and hurting person can become holy. One is in
effect withholding medicine from a needful patient, fearing
that the stick of the needle might be deemed "not nice" or
"offensive."

Fourth, the Ninth Commandment forbids bearing false
witness, which as a rubric proscribes a variety of linguistic
and behavioral abuses, all rooted in protecting real reality, or
truth-telling. The Westminster tradition draws out some of
the wider applications of the commandment:

> The sins forbidden in the ninth commandment are,
> all *prejudicing the truth*, and the good name of our
> neighbours,… *outfacing and overbearing the truth,
> concealing the truth*,… *perverting [the truth] to a wrong
> meaning*,… to the *prejudice* of *truth or justice, speaking
> untruth, lying*,…[7]

The law of God forbids speaking untruth or occluding
the truth in all its forms, including calling a man a woman.
As Paul said, "Let God be true, though every one a liar. As
it is written, That you may be justified in your words, and
prevail when you are judged" (Rom. 3:4).

---

7   Westminster Larger Catechism, Answer to Question
145: *What sins are forbidden in the ninth commandment?*

Fifth, though the confused person often cries unfairness or offense, note the manipulative asymmetry of the objection. That person seeks to impose upon and overbear the consciences of all others. The confused person is insisting that others pretend he or she is a different sex and that they thereby participate in or become complicit in this person's confusion. The people refusing to employ the wrong pronoun in contrast, however, are not similarly insisting that the confused person use the proper reality-based pronoun. Rather, those people are simply standing on reality and conscience, and aligning their vocabulary with those choices, a position perfectly consistent with human flourishing and liberty – and a Christian ethic.

Sixth, note that proper sexuality always relates to marriage,[8] as composed of one man and one woman. This frames and informs the entire biblical narrative: it is the creational norm; it marks Jesus' first public miracle; and it is the consummational norm. Marriage by creational norm and divine declaration is inherently and indispensably sexually binary. A misused pronoun in principle undermines this foundational, pre-political society by rendering both history and metaphysics as mere accidents – biology becomes bigotry. And, redefining "maleness" and "femaleness" as nothing more than preference extends well beyond the decisions and activities of "consenting adults." It means that "parent," "mother," "father," and "family" become not extant natural pre-political institutions, but mere fluid labels that become

---

8   P. Andrew Sandlin, *The Christian Sexual Worldview: God's Order in an Age of Sexual Chaos*, (Coulterville, CA: Tim Gallant Creative/ Publishing Buddy, 2015).

legitimate only through the state's fiat. Power, rather than nature, thus determines status.[9]

And, seventh, proper pronoun usage is necessarily a "gospel issue." Paul teaches that human marriage is an analogue to THE marriage of Christ, the [male] Bridegroom to the [female] Bride (2 Cor. 11:2; Eph. 5:25-27). For this analogy to work, "male" and "female" must be immutable metaphysical realities, not merely social constructs, as insisted upon by gender ideology or personal preference. The pronouns "his" and "her" and "he" and "she" thus attach to real reality; they link and refer to the immutable creational norms of "male" and "female." This is why gender ideology undermines reality and attacks the foundations of the Christian faith, it is a gospel issue. As Archbishop Chaput explains:

> In decoupling gender from biology and denying any given or "natural" meaning to male and female sexuality, gender ideology directly repudiates reality. People don't need to be "religious" to notice that men and women are different. The evidence is obvious. And, the only way to ignore it is through a kind of intellectual self-hypnosis. Gender ideology rejects any human experience of knowledge that conflicts with its own flawed premises; it's the imperialism of bad science on steroids. For Christians, it also attacks the heart of our faith: the Creation ("male and female he created them"); the Incarnation – God taking the flesh of a man; and the Redemption – God dying on the cross

---

9   See Nancy Pearcey, *Love Thy Body: Answering Hard Questions about Life and Sexuality* (Grand Rapids: Baker, 2018), 212-213.

and then rising in glorified bodily form.[10]

Who do we say people are? They are who God, the Creator and Redeemer says that they are: fearfully and wonderfully made, dignified and worthy, reflecting His very likeness and image as male and female – he and she; him and her; Bride and Groom – all to God's glory.

---

10   Charles J. Chaput, *Strangers in a Strange Land: Living the Catholic Faith in a Post-Christian World* (New York: Henry Holt and Company, 2017), 93.

THE *TRANS* MOVEMENTS AS RELIGIOUS COMMITMENT

Joseph Boot

Then God said, "Let Us make man in Our image, according to Our likeness. They will rule the fish of the sea, the birds of the sky, the livestock, all the earth, and the creatures that crawl on the earth." So God created man in His own image; He created him in the image of God; He created them male and female. God blessed them, and God said to them, "Be fruitful, multiply, fill the earth, and subdue it. (Gen. 1:26-28)

THE DENIAL OF REALITY

A person truly rooted in biblical religious commitment and the life of the Christian family has an established identity that is based in reality, and is therefore very hard to manipulate or control. Imposing an abstract ideology designed to remake the world on such a person is nearly impossible. They are not part of 'mass man' governed by the abstraction of elite opinion. The spiritual and moral bond of commitment to God in Christ and the social bond of the family provides a vital foundation that must be shattered if people are to be seduced into a world of expressive individualism, sexual gratification and self-definition. In her outstanding work, *The Global Sexual Revolution*, Gabriele Kuby lays out the stakes and implications of our subject for human culture:

> As sex goes, so goes the family; as the family goes, so goes society…if this model [lifelong marriage and family] is undermined through constant mass sexualization and a hollowing-out and distorting of the concept of marriage and family, then the foundation on which the culture rests is destroyed.[1]

The undermining of that foundation is now far advanced in our society. We find ourselves in a surreal world of 'trans' ideologies today where certain people uninterested in the given realities of *human* life are determined to overturn every distinction set out in the Word of God in creation and Scripture, and consequently the vital fabric of our culture is being shredded. This is occurring both in relation to real distinctions between men and women, but also with respect to the fundamental distinction between the animal and human, the human and machine.

For those in any doubt, a recent article in the Canadian media caught my attention. A female Canadian powerlifter, April Hutchinson, is facing a two-year suspension from her sport by the Canadian Powerlifting Union for voicing con-

---

1   Gabriele Kuby, *The Global Sexual Revolution: Destruction of Freedom in the Name of Freedom* (Kettering: LifeSite, 2015), 40, 175.

cerns that men masquerading as women were dominating and ruining female powerlifting competitions. This fact is well documented. Recently a Canadian 'transgender' athlete who is a biological male has been setting multiple records in the female division, shattering the women's world record by beating his closest female competitor by a massive 200 kilograms.[2] It is one thing for the man concerned to live in his delusion with any degree of self-respect, it is another for professional bodies to take such athletes and records seriously. Hutchinson commented:

> I now face a 2-year ban by the CPU for speaking publicly about the unfairness of biological males being allowed to taunt female competitors and loot their winnings. Apparently, I have failed in my gender-role duties as 'supporting actress' in the horror show that is my sport right now.[3]

The absurdity of this situation beggars all belief and yet this is where we are in Western cultural life. A recent book on the Sexual Revolution by a leading young feminist, Lou-

2   Madeline Coggins, 'Trans Athlete Sparks Outrage After Toppling Women's Powerlifting World Record,' *Fox Business*, https://www.foxbusiness.com/politics/trans-athlete-sparks-outrage-toppling-womens-powerlifting-world-record-completely-unfair#:~:text=Her%20total%20weight%20lifted%20in,who%20finished%20at%20387.5%20kilograms, accessed November 2023.

3   Clare Marie Merkowsky 'Canadian Female Powerlifted Faces two-year Suspension for Criticizing Men Competing Against Women,' *LifeSite News*, https://www.lifesitenews.com/news/canadian-female-powerlifter-suspension-men-competing/, accessed November 2023.

ise Perry, who is not a Christian, offers a scathing critique of the irrational denial of inescapable differences between men and women. With respect to the physiological differences and referring copiously to various scientific studies, she writes:

> Adult women are approximately half as strong as adult men in the upper body and two-thirds as strong in the lower body. On average men can bench press more mass than women can by a factor of roughly two and a half and can punch harder by a similar factor. In hand grip strength, 90% of females produce less force than 95% of males. In other words, almost all women are weaker than almost all men, and any feminist analysis of the power dynamic between men and women has to begin with the recognition of this fact. And men can out-run women…At the 2016 Summer Olympics, for instance, Elaine Thompson of Jamaica won gold with a time of 10.71 seconds…she would have been easily out-run by Jamaican boys competing in the under-seventeen category, just as the United States women's national football team in 2017 were beaten by the Dallas under-fifteen boys' team. The women's category has traditionally been protected in elite sports because, if it were not protected, there would be no women in elite sports.[4]

This statement is, for the vast majority of people, just a reflection of common sense and as uncontroversial as it

---

4   Louise Perry, *The Case Against the Sexual Revolution: A New Guide to Sex in the 21ˢᵗ Century* (Cornwall: Polity Press, 2022), 27-28.

would have been to people in the Victorian age. However, radical feminist ideologues, quickly followed by queer Critical Theorists, have been determined to overturn these realities in the abstract world of academia; this new academic orthodoxy has now been imposed upon the real world, whilst actual women working in professional sports have strongly opposed them. As anti-Christian worldviews are pushed to this self-conscious and logical extreme, the question that is taking centre stage is that of distinction, or what we might also refer to as transcendence.

THE MAKER'S INSTRUCTIONS

The Christian scholar Hans Jurgen Baden in the last century perceived that:

> The coming religious controversy will no longer take place on the basis of the logical *pro* and *contra*, but on a basis which grips man utterly. It will change from the sphere of the word and of words into the sphere of *being and life-form*. The final legitimation of the truth lies in the possibility of its incarnation.[5]

It is hard to overstate the prophetic character of this insight. In our generation in the West, the bounds of acceptable speech have shifted from the sphere of logical argument for and against biblical faith, to an attempt to redefine reality itself and incarnate a new word in terms of a new *mode of*

---

5   Hans Jurgen Baden, cited in Denzil G.M. Patrick, *Pascal & Kierkegaard: A Study Strategy in Evangelism* (Cambridge: James Clarke & Co, 1947), 395.

being and life-form; a de-creation followed by self-creation.

In the scriptures, the foundation for a biblical world and life view begins with the first chapter of the book of beginnings which sets out the crucial distinction between absolute *creator* and the *creature* – relative created being. Genesis then addresses the unique nature of the human person, as well as the ineradicable normative distinctions within creation – darkness and light, land and sea, plant and animal life as distinct from man himself (Gen. 1). There is no true parallel to the creation account in Genesis or its Christological deepening in the first chapter of John's gospel anywhere in human thought, and without it there is no envisioning of Western civilization. We are told in Genesis that the most important thing to know about human beings is that they are *made in the image of God* – that is, our nature as beings in accountable relation to another – and that we are made *male and female*. Critically, we are taught that this necessary creational structure is life-giving, life-affirming and has in view a specific cultural task in God's economy for history (Gen. 1:28).

This is the starting point of God's fundamental order for creation revealed in Torah. The term Torah is translated as 'law' or 'instruction' – a word which reminds us that we are *in-structure, in-relationship* and therefore accountable. Ours is not a structureless, lawless world, but existence in-relation to a personal God whose Word to and for creation constitutes both meaning and order. It is only within this context that human beings, the *pinnacle* of that creational theatre, are enabled to flourish and find fulfillment.

Perhaps unsurprisingly, poets have reflected with marvel

on the lords of creation. Shakespeare's Hamlet says:

> What a piece of work is a man! how noble in reason!
> how infinite in faculty! in form and moving how express
> and admirable! in action how like an angel! in appre-
> hension how like a god! the beauty of the world! the
> paragon of animals! And yet, to me, what is this quin-
> tessence of dust?

The Psalmist, under the inspiration of the Holy Spirit,
likewise wonders at God's image-bearer:

> …what is man that You remember him,
> the son of man that You look after him?
> You made him little less than God
> and crowned him with glory and honor.
> You made him lord over the works of Your hands;
> You put everything under His feet:
> all the sheep and oxen,
> as well as the animals in the wild,
> > the birds of the sky,
> > and the fish of the sea
> > that pass through the currents of the seas. (Psalm
> > 8:4-8).

The glory, beauty and dignity of humanity is therefore
seen in both our relatedness to God *and* our role in creation
to live *coram deo* (before the face of God) with a task for
which we are each accountable. The problem of course is
the fallenness and pride of man in sin and rebellion against

God. His will to be his own god is a defiant lurch toward death in the attempt to alienate creation from its maker by overturning its normative structure and vainly seeking to use our creaturely freedoms to thwart its movement toward total restoration and renewal.

THE TRANS*GENDER* MOVEMENT

Inevitably, how a society answers the question 'who is man?' determines the direction of that culture and the lives of the individuals in it. The political demolition of sexual norms brought about by the Sexual Revolution was inescapably rooted in the underlying question of the nature of human beings, and the answer was given in atheistic, Freudian, and Marxian terms. With the biblical view discarded, the genie was out of the bottle. As Carl Trueman explains:

> The acceptance of Freud's basic insight, that *sexual desire is constitutive of identity*, and this from infancy onwards, is therefore an anthropological, philosophical and political watershed. To concede this point means that debates about the limits of acceptable sexual expression become almost pointless because any attempt to corral sexual behaviour is then rendered an oppressive move designed to make the individual inauthentic...attempts to set limits based on the intrinsic nature of certain sexual acts are ultimately arbitrary and politically motivated.[6]

---

6   Carl R. Trueman, *The Rise and Triumph of the Modern Self: Cultural Amnesia, Expressive Individualism and the Road to Sexual Revolution* (Illinois: Crossway, 2020), 264.

For neo-Marxists then, sexual identity is a political matter, because any form of sexual discipline and direction, social or legal, is interpreted as *oppression*. All forms of sexual deviance then require *liberation* in the form of a psychosexual politics that emerges from various Critical Theories – that is, theories that liberate from the oppressive structures of the Christian order.

This emancipation is not only from so-called traditional mores of sexual restraint within the bond of marriage, rather it is the attempt to throw off *every form* of structural limitation on human autonomy:

> Modern and post-modern man have emancipated themselves – from God, from nature, from the family, from tradition – woman from man, children from parents and individuals from themselves as man or woman. They stand naked, restrained by nothing and defined by nothing other than their own wishes, desires and drives. They think they are free to self-actualize, and do not notice that, in their vulnerability and lack of inhibitions, they are more malleable than ever before.[7]

Clearly, this is no longer simply a matter of old-fashioned promiscuity or even of just male homosexuality and lesbianism. The new expressive individualism seeks only inner psychological well-being by stripping away all moral, cultural and biologically structured norms in order to make space for a true noble savage to emerge. Biology itself with its gender binary must be overcome and a 'queer'

---

7   Gabriele Kuby, *The Global Sexual Revolution*, 174.

psychologized idea of sex and gender is to replace it. In the therapeutic society, sex (your biological reality) is separated from gender (your self-actualizing psychological self) so that either-or (binary) gender norms are effectively eliminated.

For radical theorists like Judith Butler, who influenced a generation of intellectuals to think this way (cf. *Gender Trouble*), your gender is simply *performance* – to act like a man or woman – it has no ontological status in creation. There is no created male or female 'being' behind the performative doing, no gender identity before gender expressions.[8] You are not born a man or woman but become such, or neither. The ideas of man and woman, male and female, are the fictive creations of language repetition. Marriage is a social construct, a political power play in the interests of white, male, heterosexual capitalists. Changing the language game is therefore the essence of politics toward the remaking of social reality.

The fact is that the concrete reality of being a woman, of childbearing and all that this presupposes in terms of real biological essence is ignored by Butler as a lesbian, who believes that in the abstract private world of her personal psychology, she transcends the categories of male or female. Thus, as Trueman correctly notes, 'transgenderism is merely the latest iteration of self-creation that becomes necessary in the wake of decreation.'[9]

---

8   Judith Butler, *Gender Trouble*, (New York: Routledge, 1990), 25-26.

9   Trueman, *The Rise and Triumph*, 363.

The Trans*humanist* Movement

An important reality largely unexplored in this context is the relationship between *transgenderism* and *transhumanism* – both of which, as developments within Western thinking on selfhood, believe that people can transition and transcend, by our own psychological and technological power, the bounds of created human nature. For example, LGBTQQIP2SA, represents Lesbian, Gay, Bisexual, Transgender, Queer, Questioning, Intersex, Pansexual, Two-Spirited, and Asexual. This ever-evolving acronym reflects a refusal to conform to created reality. In my view transgenderism is a form of transhumanism sharing the same basic assumptions. Transgenderism only has a degree of acceptability and plausibility today because of its spiritually popular *de-creation narrative* and the advance of human technique – being facilitated by the *technological ability* to artificially manipulate and impersonate biological realities.

Transhumanism is at root a religious worldview in which man self-consciously seeks to become a god, remaking himself in a new image. Rooted in atheistic materialism, the movement 'projects a new phase in evolutionary history on the basis of the use of technology.'[10] In a promotional video for a transhumanist Global Future Congress in New York, this new era for humanity is set out:

> What we need is not just a new technological revolution but a new civilization or paradigm; we need a new philosophy and ideology, new ethics, new culture, new

---

10   Henk G. Geertsema, *Homo Respondens: Essays in Christian Philosophy* (Ontario: Paideia Press, 2021), 319.

psychology and even a new metaphysics. We must reset our limits and go beyond ourselves, beyond the earth and beyond the solar system...thus a new reality and future man will arise.[11]

Leading transhumanist thinker Natasha Vita-More drafted a transhumanist manifesto in 1994 in which she asserts that as our ideas and tools continue to evolve, so shall we – both in terms of our bodies and values. The goal is more than the enhancement of the body and its senses but a world of 'diversity and multiplicity' with transhuman rights of 'morphological freedom.'[12] This is the 'freedom' to alter and change the body and the very nature of human beings.

Transhumanism aims finally at the creation of a *cyborg* – a cybernetically controlled organism where the person no longer simply utilizes but *merges* with human technology. In science fiction there have been both positive and negative portrayals of this ideal. In *Star Trek the Motion Picture* (the first Star Trek film in 1979) the story revolves around the discovery of a self-conscious machine that is searching for the creator. It turns out that the machine is the twentieth-century earth satellite Voyager which, having gathered knowledge for centuries in terms of its original programing, became self-conscious and now wants to find the creator to fulfill its purpose of delivering that information. The movie ends with a lead character *merging* with the machine and

11   '2045: A New Era for Humanity' (May 2013), cited in David Herbert: *Becoming God: Transhumanism and the Quest for Cybernetic Immortality* (Ontario: Joshua Press, 2014), 139-140.

12   Natasha Vita-More, cited in David Herbert, *Becoming God*, 122.

the birth of a new immortal species.

Although indirectly raising interesting questions about the human search for God – picked up in Star Trek V, *The Final Frontier* – the vital point is that *man* is the creator and merging with his own technology becomes a godlike being shattering all human and biological limitations. This film offers an idealistic picture of the glorious future of humanity merging with its own creation. Similarly, more recent films like the 2014 movie *Transcendence* offer an explicitly posthuman message with technology represented as offering divine transcendence. The lead character, an artificial intelligence scientist, passes away, but his wife uploads his consciousness into a quantum computer and connects it to the internet.

By contrast, in the later Star Trek film *First Contact* (1996), a subsequent generation with a new Enterprise ship and crew encounters the quintessential embodiment of the cyborg in an alien race known as the Borg (the name riffing off cyborg). The Borg are a hive mind, there are no true individuals, but the Borg collective consciousness is manifested in separate humanoid drones, supposedly superior entities seamlessly combining the organic with the synthetic. They forcibly assimilate organic species into their collective, incorporating their biological and technological distinctives with their own in the pursuit of perfection and immortality. Here, although human beings are merged with technology transcending their biological limitations, existence as a cyborg is depicted in nightmarish and dystopian terms where all that is truly human – personal identity, self-determination, creative thought, freedom and indeed human imperfection is abolished. This film offers a negative appraisal of transhuman aspirations.

Today, with the popularity and developments in Artificial Intelligence and the notable hysteria surrounding it, metaphysical questions regarding the distinction between the human and machine are being raised – some even suggesting the distinction is breaking down. However, as Henk Geertsema has pointed out, the machine, no matter how sophisticated, is just a *physical device* designed by humans to perform certain functions, 'Technological developments in relation to human and machine do not warrant the use of *cyborg* as a symbol for a boundary evasion between them.'[13]

The reductionistic *physicalism* involved in the transhumanist view inevitably tries to reduce self-awareness, human choice, emotion as well as ethical and legal accountability to purely *physical* phenomenon – potentially downloadable into another substrate (i.e., a computer of some kind), because the human organism and machine are considered merely materialistically as information processing devices. The outcome is that the very idea of truly *mental* causes (that cannot be reduced to physics) is destroyed, along with notions of individual human personhood and their freedom.

Just as the origin story of transgenderism must reject the biblical account of male and female created in God's image as original normative distinct identities, so the cyborg story of transhumanism must deny not only the unique creation of human persons whose life is more than physics through animation by the very breath of God (Gen. 2:7), it must

13   Geertsema, *Homo Respondens*, 325.

also dispense with any notion of the fall of human beings into sin and ruin and their need to be restored. Instead, the new cyborg ontology has its own eschatology. Denis Alexander, Director of the Faraday Institute for Science and Religion at Cambridge University articulates the religious hope of transhumanism:

> The messianic hope in this case is placed in technology that will shape the enhanced, better human, perhaps a new species altogether, the posthuman. And then in the far future lies the hope of immortality when the posthuman will become substrate independent, delivered from the constraints of flesh and blood to live on in a digital heaven.[14]

Combining an allegedly *objective* scientific method (destroying freedom) with the *subjective* projection of the inner self (destroying law-order), in both transgenderism and transhumanism we encounter the radical autonomy of the individual from God, expressed in its socialistic form, 'freedom over against oppression, inclusivity over against exclusion. Cyborg becomes the icon of protest against fixed oppositions.'[15] In short, out with the distinction between the divine and human, male and female, man and machine – all such oppositions are oppression! With no original integrity or unity to a creation that has fallen and been disrupted requiring restoration and redemption, the cyborg concept of remaking human nature by technique becomes

14   Denis Alexander, cited in Herbert, *Becoming God*, 138.
15   Geertsema, *Homo Respondens*, 351.

a political myth that seeks to take the place of the biblical worldview. Human organization, planning, technique and technology will bring humanity to new birth, manipulate reality to fulfil our desires, and save us from despair. The political myth thus becomes a religious myth of salvation.

THE GARDEN OF GOD

Responding faithfully to the *trans* religious myth requires us not only to analyze its content but to notice with compassionate understanding the struggle to find the self, and the true fulfilment of this struggle in Christ Jesus alone. Geertsema has insightfully pointed out that:

> Our sense of personal identity does not start to develop out of an inner subjectivity, even less out of scientific knowledge; it begins as a *response* to somebody who relates to me as a person.[16]

In the garden of God, Adam and Eve as male and female were placed in the immediacy of personal relationship to God and to each other. In the context of this relationship, they were given responsibility to *freely form* creation in a cultural task for which the entire human family is accountable (Gen. 1:26-28; 2:15-17, 21-25). This responsibility and accountability to a personal God who made us for fellowship with Himself *is the essence of life's meaning* and basis of human identity from the Christian standpoint. In the biblical world and life view, the first humans used this freedom to distance themselves from God by seeking to be-

16   Geertsema, *Homo Respondens*, 354.

come their own god (Gen 3:5). And so, the Lord God came looking for a *response* from the couple He had created and animated in spiritual relation to Himself calling out, 'where art thou?' (Gen. 3:9). Critically, in this fall from right relation to his creator, man lost not only the living God but *himself.* Interestingly, this finds initial expression with our first parents trying to cover their sexual identities in the grip of shame. By human *technique* in the sewing of fig leaves, they hid from God and each other (Gen. 3:7-10). From this time on, human beings have wrestled with an identity crisis.

It is clear from Genesis and the rest of Scripture that human sin, alienation and the subsequent loss of the self is not simply a problem of the intellect, but of the heart and will (Prov. 4:23) – a problem of *defiance* (Gen. 3:1-6; Matt. 15:18-20; Rom. 8:6-8). This spiritual reality is well expressed in a poem of the young Karl Marx:

> In a prayer of despair, I will build myself a throne.
> Cold and huge will be its summit,
> Its bulwark will be superhuman horror,
> And its marshal will be gloomy agony.[17]

Because God created human image-bearers as a 'relation,' the only true *ground* of the self is the Triune God who is in eternal relation to Himself. To try to find or define the self apart from this relation to God is a form of *despair* – and its outcome is only agony and horror. The subjective

---

17   Karl H. Marx, "Invocation of One in Despair," *All Poetry,* https://allpoetry.com/Invocation-Of-One-In-Despair, retrieved November 2023.

freedom and independence of the human person that we experience is only a creaturely and relative freedom – which is to say it is a created freedom, temporal, embodied and historical. We can never be God, remaking reality after our image. Unlike God we are not self-established (self-defining – I am that I am), we cannot create ourselves out of nothing. We are 'selves' established by another.

REFLECTING ON OURSELVES

To understand the root of transgenderism and transhumanism it is important to notice that as self-conscious beings we are able to step back from ourselves and reflect on who we are – in this sense we *relate to ourselves*. As we do, we encounter the self we *are* and have *become*, as well as the self we hope to be and strive to become, the one we *project*. Because as creatures we always relate to ourselves by relation to something other and higher (outside the self), there are ultimately only *two paths* for understanding ourselves: we either accept that we have an identity established by our creator and so choose to truly be our created selves by living in accountability *coram deo* – before the face of God - , or we choose to 'be as god' and imagine we can establish ourselves by relating to a different criterion. This alternate criterion might be the state or society, an ideal of the same or opposite sex, a given sexual desire, an abstract principle or human technique; any number of things may offer an alternate basis for establishing the self. However, because God alone is the true criterion of the self, these idols, being a false measure, lead only to confusion and agony.

The existentialist philosopher Jean-Paul Sartre realised that human beings 'are a choice and for us, to be is to choose ourselves.'[18] But rather than choosing ourselves as created and intended by our maker, Sartre alleged that human consciousness is an attempt to *become God* – to be totally original and create *de novo*. Admitting this was impossible, he despaired, saying, 'man is a useless passion.'[19] Whenever human beings fail to become themselves in relation to the living God by trying to ground and construct their identity in God substitutes, ruin is the inevitable result. Scripture identifies the attempt to define ourselves and our lives in this way as sin.

THE NATURE OF DESPAIR

We hear a great deal in our present culture about 'authenticity' and 'being yourself' or expressing yourself, and in one sense the Christian can agree that we *must* be ourselves. Indeed, God calls us to become our unique selves in terms of His purposes. Even though we belong to the human family, we are not exhausted by the abstract unity of *humanity* as though we are each simply one example of a species like an earthworm or ant. As God says to the prophet Jeremiah:

The word of the Lord came to me:

I chose you before I formed you in the womb;

I set you apart before you were born.

I appointed you a prophet to the nations. (Jer. 1:4-5)

---

18   Jean-Paul Sartre, *The Wisdom of Jean-Paul Satre* (New York: Philosophical Library, 1956), 40.

19   Jean-Paul Sartre, *Being and Nothingness*, trans, Hazel E. Barnes (New York: Washington Square, 1992), 754.

In a similar fashion the Psalmist writes:

> For it was You who created my inward parts;
> You knit me together in my mother's womb.
> I will praise You
> because I have been remarkably and wonderfully made.
> Your works are wonderful,
> and I know this very well...
> Your eyes saw me when I was formless;
> all my days were written in Your book and planned
> before a single one of them began. (Ps. 139:13, 14, 16)

The scriptures are clear that we are uniquely made with a purpose and plan in mind. The apostle Paul tells us that God the Father is the source, 'from whom every family in heaven and on earth is named' (Eph. 3:15). We might say that we each have a divine name; God has defined our being. This is the *givenness* of the self, the aspect of necessity. We were all intended, called forth, wanted, loved, with a specific calling to become and do that for which we were made. Yet, both the prophet Jeremiah and king David had to choose to become themselves – they did not arrive in the world fully actualized as prophet or king. They grew and developed, choosing their course amidst possibility, and they sinned and grappled with despair.

Recognizing that sin leads people to despair is important for understanding our culture and sharing the truth of the gospel with those in the grip of *trans* ideologies. A helpful guide in this regard is the Danish Christian thinker, Soren Kierkegaard, who lived and wrote in the nineteenth century long before *trans* movements ever emerged. He argued that despair is not simply an emotion, but a *condition* a person lives in – in that sense despair *is sin* by refusing to choose to be the person God created you to be, and it manifests itself in a variety of different ways. We have all at times lived in despair because it is the *misrelation* of ourselves to God, to our own being, and to others – all sin has the character of a misrelation. As human beings, male and female, we are spiritual beings oriented to our maker, with eternity in our hearts (Eccl. 3:11), yet at the same time we are each placed in a particular time, family, and context to fulfil an historical calling. As creatures, the self is therefore partly a *given*, but is not perfectly or fully *actualized*. We grow and develop, accountable in the context of God's order, as we confront possibility and choice. It is here in the realm of both possibility and necessity that we flounder.

In his book *The Sickness unto Death*, Kierkegaard helps us to understand the specific nature of despair. In particular, what he calls the *despair of defiance* is helpful for understanding and responding to *trans* ideologies. In this despairing state, a person, recognizing that the self is a *task* or calling, wills to be a self, but not the true self they were created to be. Instead, they demand to decide for themselves who they are and who they are to become. This defiance can be the result of being overwhelmed by a sense of *infinite possibility*, whilst throwing off the constraints of *finite necessity*. However, as Kierkegaard puts it, 'Actuality is a *unity* of possibility and necessity.'[20] That is, human flourishing

---

20 Soren Kierkegaard, *The Sickness unto Death, Kierkegaard's Writings 19*. Trans. Howard V. Hong and Edna H. Hong (Princeton:

requires both possibility and necessity and where either is denied, we live in despair. The person in the grip of *necessity*, for example, becomes fatalistic, deterministic and so narrow that they lack the courage to break out of conformity to the spirits of the world – they never discover who they were made and called to be.

However, of particular relevance for the *trans* movements is the despair of *possibility*. When we lose sight of our created finitude and the *givenness* of our personhood, our God-given imagination becomes an end in itself and life starts to be lived through a kind of inner fantasy, leading us away from ourselves. In other words, where we lack a proper sense of created divine necessity, the reality of possibility runs wild and unrestrained. Stephen Evans points to the illustration of oxygen in understanding this possibility:

> A human person cannot breathe and thus cannot live without oxygen, but it is also impossible to breathe pure oxygen. Similarly, the self cannot breathe as spirit without possibility, though it is impossible to live on possibility alone.[21]

The person claiming to be *transgendered*, in desperately seeking to find the self in an ideal of the opposite sex or the abstract fiction of gender fluidity, is trying to breathe pure oxygen (i.e., pure possibility), and has become tragically

Princeton University Press, 1980), 36.

21   C. Stephen Evans, *Kierkegaard and Spirituality: Accountability as the Meaning of Human Existence* (Grand Rapids: Eerdmans, 2019), 26.

lost in the imagination. Whilst believing they are becoming *more real*, by choosing themselves in relation to an idol, they lose contact with the necessary structure of their created self, and so the self becomes increasingly *unreal*. The same can be said for the *transhumanist* who, gripped in the imagination by the myth of self-creation reaches for infinitude and immortality through pure possibility and the dream of defying all necessity by an apostate use of the gift of free formation – in this case technology. Both refuse to obey or submit to their limitations and the necessary conditions of life.[22]

BECOMING YOURSELF

The situation is one of a tragic *parody*. In one sense, unlike many less thoughtful people, *trans* movements are sufficiently self-conscious and spiritually aware to understand that human beings have a freedom and responsibility to be and choose themselves, but they do so in the sin of open defiance against their maker. Kierkegaard prophetically saw that such a person refuses to begin 'at the beginning' but seeks a godlike absoluteness to start 'in the beginning':

> [T]he self in despair wants to be master of himself or to create himself, to make his self into the self he wants to be, to determine what he will have or not have in his concrete self.[23]

The tragedy however is that all such ephemeral choices are arbitrary because, lacking contact with one's God-given

---

22 Kierkegaard, *The Sickness*, 36.
23 Kierkegaard, *The Sickness*, 68.

self, they have no stability and can always come apart and be undone for the person to try and reinvent themselves all over again. For those whose change of mind is because of *God's claim* on their true self, like those who wish to de-transition after horrific surgeries in a hopeless attempt to match their bodies to their imagination, they have to live with the damage done. Those who promote and propagate *trans* ideologies are thus like kings without a country because logically rebellion is legitimate at any moment. The illusion of absolute freedom makes for an empty self and empty life.[24]

I called the *trans idea* a tragic parody, a hopeless striving, because we have seen it is a creation myth as well as a story that impersonates being born again – whether into new sexual identity or by merging with technology. It is a form of spirituality, but it is a *demonic* form because of its self-conscious rebellion. But when God reveals Himself in Jesus Christ to a person, the despair of defiance is exposed for the sin it is and the only *resolution* is brought to light in the genuine *recreation* offered through repentance and faith in the atoning death and resurrection life of the eternal Son who made us for relationship with Himself. He offers new life and new birth, abolishing death and bringing immortality to light, satisfying all our infinite longings (2 Tim. 1:10). Christ Jesus offers true rest for the self by bringing to an end to the wearisome struggle for identity. The Saviour's gentle yoke of *necessity* makes sense of our human *possibility*:

"Come to Me, all of you who are weary and burdened,

---

24   See, Evans, *Kierkegaard*, 38.

and I will give you *rest*. All of you, take up My yoke and learn from Me, because I am gentle and humble in heart, and you will find rest for *yourselves*. For My yoke is easy and My burden is light" (Matt. 11:28-30)

It is in the Son of God and Son of man, our creator *and* brother that we discover who we truly are, and through whom we are finally liberated to be ourselves. In the words of C. S Lewis, '…it will never be lawful simply to "be ourselves" until "ourselves" have become sons of God....[25]

25   C.S. Lewis, *God in the Dock* (Grand Rapids: Eerdmans, 1972), 286.

FROM OLD-FASHIONED PAGAN MASCULINITY TO POSTMODERN MACHISMO AND THE NEW MISOGYNY

P. Andrew Sandlin

Ideological feminists and other modern Leftists routinely accuse biblical Christians and sociopolitical conservatives of misogyny on account of their support for biblical or traditional male-female distinctions. The guiding tenet of contemporary Leftism is egalitarianism,[1] particularly sexual egalitarianism, which demands across-the-board equality of men and women. This is not *legal* equality (which has been pervasive in the West for many decades and reflects the biblical view), but *existential* equality — the assumption that there are no ontologically rooted differences between men and women that dictate some distinct callings and roles. In the creation order man and woman are equally made in God's image, equally valuable in his sight, and equally charged with stewarding his creation — but are not called to do all things equally. That divinely established natural order (in biblical terms, *creation*) must yield to the Leftist utopian dream that differences between men and women

1   Kenneth Minogue, *The Servile Mind* (New York and London: Encounter Books), 2010, 296.

93

are mere social constructions invented by a hegemonic patriarchy, and can be remedied by modern monstrosities like womb-encasing males and phalloplasty-re-engineered females. The fact that anybody with two eyes can discern there are obvious and insurmountable differences between men and women which no surgery can mask or erase has done nothing to impede the bizarre Leftist ideology at war with the cosmos. The cosmos will win that war.

Since this Leftist egalitarianism has gained the upper hand in Western culture, and in fact has been the leading political component of the larger Sexual Revolution since the 1960s, we should not be surprised at the emergence of a conservative counter-revolution reasserting male-female differences and traditional social hierarchies. The impulses behind this reaction are warranted: sexual egalitarianism assaults God's creational order and sows social chaos. However, since the counter-revolutionaries are usually not guided by the Word of God but by alien, worldly presuppositions, they offer no cure for the disease and in some cases their alternative proposal is every bit as injurious as the disease itself. An ingenious insight of Christian philosopher Herman Dooyeweerd is that apostate thought always swings between a "dialectic" of opposing poles that absolutize some aspect of the temporal order. Since apostates deny the absoluteness of the Word of God, they have only the shifting sand of the temporal world on which to stand.[2] They end up with one foot planted and then quickly unsettled, only to plant a foot in the opposite direction, with equally unsettling results.

---

2   Herman Dooyeweerd, *Roots of Western Culture* (Ancaster, Ontario, Canada: Paideia Press, 2012), 12–15.

The Leftist egalitarianism and the conservative counter-revolution are equally futile attempts at a foothold in quicksand.

Since, in review, Leftist egalitarianism is based in modern secularism, the conservative counter-revolutionaries looks around for alternative foundations resisting it. Since they refuse to submit to the Word of God, they are open to alien alternatives just as spurious as secularism. Once of them is ancient paganism. Enter the Bronze Age Mindset.

THE BRONZE AGE MINDSET

Bronze Age Mindset (BAM) is both a book[3] and movement targeting young white right-wing males. The author (who also hosts a wildly popular X [formerly Twitter] account) designates himself the anonymous Bronze Age Pervert. He has since been widely identified as the Romanian-American far-right figure Costin Vlad Alamariu. He holds a Ph.D. from Yale and his dissertation was titled "The Problem of Tyranny and Philosophy in the Thought of Plato and Nietzsche." The BAM Wikipedia entry states (with supporting documentation):

> *Bronze Age Mindset* gained a cult following in right-wing circles including staffers of the Trump White House and on Capitol Hill, according to anonymous sources described by *Politico* and *Huffington Post*. *National Review* writer Nate Hochman claims that many of his peers who read the book and [Michael] Anton's review

---

3   Independently published, 2018. I'm working from the Kindle edition.

of it [in the *Claremont Review of Books*] ended up interning at the Claremont Institute, and asks, "Why did every junior staffer in the Trump administration read 'Bronze Age Mindset?' There was something there that was clearly attractive to young conservative elites." In the summer of 2018 it was among the top 150 books sold on Amazon sitewide, which is notable according to Anton and Dan DeCarlo since it was achieved without the aid of a publicist or book deal. In October 2019, it was still ranked third in Ancient Greek History and #174 in Humour on the Amazon best-seller list.

BAM romanticizes, embellishes, and seeks to revive the spirit of the ancient pagan world in countering the evils of modern Western civilization, which it sees as terminally diseased and fit only for a quick and violent death. Christians who have correctly pinpointed the emergence of neopaganism from the Left,[4] notably in its sexually egalitarian feature, might be surprised at the seemingly out-of-nowhere emergence of a competing right-wing version. But BAM is every bit as pagan as Leftist neopaganism and by far more explicit. The book is a rambling, punchy, raunchy, occasionally intellectually coherent argument against modernity; against feminism; against human equality of all sorts; and, notably, against biblical Christianity. To BAM, the hope for humanity is a revival of a very pagan past.

---

4   See Peter Jones, *Capturing the Pagan Mind* (Nashville, Tennessee: Broadman & Holman, 2003).

THE BRONZE AGE MALES

The vanguard of that pagan revival is a cadre of robust, muscle-bound, beautiful young males animated by the "life-force" of nature. BAM is animist (a supernatural principle pervades all life), pantheist (god is nature itself), and vitalist (life is dependent on a principle beyond chemical or physical forces). It holds that to deny the one God is not to deny the gods. Indeed, the beautiful young white muscular males will themselves become the new gods ("[m]any of the Greek heroes and gods had fair hair and blue or grey eyes," Alamariu alerts the reader). They will cultivate their deity by "sun and steel": lying in the sun every day and soaking up its health-producing power, and in fact, becoming sun-worshipers. In tandem they must take up a regimen of weightlifting to enhance the godlike beauty of their physique. "Only physical beauty," Alamariu opines, "is the foundation for a true higher culture of the mind and spirit as well. Only sun [worship] and steel [weightlifting] will show you the path." Beautiful male bodies are the pinnacle of nature, "the body in its glorious and divine beauty." In this Bronze world, females are subordinate creatures whose consummation of sexual desire drains young males of life-force. Therefore, girlfriends and marriage should at best be a tangent, necessary evil. Life's real focus should be the formation of a camaraderie of young white muscular pirates and the domination of all inferiors, that is, all who are not other Bronze Age Males.

Pirates? Yes. They do not support themselves by work or vocation, but rather by piracy — they pillage and take at will. Work and sweat and toil are debasing; the pirate is the original form of the "free man." They revel in a world they create, a world of absolute freedom on which they impose their will to power. Parents must, therefore, allow sons freedom from any oversight to express their life-force in our otherwise decadent world. Eventually, they will grow up to create a white ethnostate of their own, separate from the rest of human civilization, which they will visit occasionally to solve its recurrent problems and to exert their inexorable will. Let it never be supposed, therefore, that utopianism is an exclusively Leftist concept. BAM is right-wing pagan utopianism at its zenith.

The ultimate cause of all modern decadence is feminism, Alamariu contends, and we live in a "gynocracy," the rule of women. The only way out of this "absolute hell" and "iron prison" of modernity is a reversion to ancient pagan animas and pantheism, recognizing that the basic truth of humanity is the life-force we must cultivate in impressionable but spiritually, psychologically, and sociologically hungry young men.

Modifying Darwin and Aping Nietzsche

BAM argues a modified Darwinist, almost entirely Nietzschean, view of history. Alamariu agrees entirely with Darwin's naturalism that the world is nothing but materiality. However, he accuses Darwin and Darwinists of lacking the courage of their convictions in the reluctance to support their survival of the fittest thesis as it consistently applies to humans. Of course, the original Social Darwinism in its commitment to eugenics was more consistent and courageous, though insufficiently so. BAM, by contrast, champions a Darwinist teleology (design toward a goal). Nature itself has its own goal, the triumph of superior humans, that is, young, beautiful, muscular white males. That is the Darwinism the Bronze Age Males must revive and commandeer.

In the Bronze Age mindset, history is not a natural progression from benightedness to enlightenment. Rather, as Nietzsche believed, it is cyclical. We will always have the enlightened and unenlightened with us, and the ancient world was populated by wiser and more enlightened individuals than exist today ("supermen"). This is why BAM espouses reincarnation. The conscious goal of the BAM is to revive their spirit. "Because of reincarnation," he declares, "greatness can be instantaneously reborn." Therefore, though naturalistic, BAM must advocate vitalism: the very old theory that a mysterious life principle within the natural order relentlessly impels it toward a self-sustaining and -perpetuating goal. BAM attempts to solve its paradox of holding simultaneously to both naturalism and teleology (how can a purely materialistic nature possibly have a design or goal?) by suggesting that while humans are biologically determined, we are still responsible because there *is* no one else to be responsible. There is nothing but nature, yet nature always favours Bronze Age Males, destined for world domination. This is the teleology and eschatology of BAM. We cannot successfully fight nature, but we can harness it.

BAM apes Nietzsche in insisting there is no transcendent morality given by God or his revelation in either creation or the Bible. The only morality is biological hierarchy. The superior humans, the supermen, impose their will on the rest of the world. In the Bible, the basic human impulse is the God-given cultural mandate (Gen. 1:28–30), exercising benevolent dominion over the non-human creation under God's authority and for his glory. For the youthful Bronze Age Males, the cultural mandate is perverted into the quest for more "living space." Young men need room to exercise their superiority, and they expropriate it as warriors akin to ancient pirates. (This sounds precisely like the rationale for war in most traditional societies.)

The BAM epistemology (view of knowledge) reflects the deep imprint of Nietzsche. The intellect is simply an expression of will, which is a concentration of life-force. Channeling the Nazi court philosopher Martin Heidegger, Alamariu writes, "Direct perception is already intellectualized." He means that how we perceive things is determined by the kind of being we are. The more of the life-force we concentrate and cultivate, the more we perceive the world as it really is. We do not experience the world and then interpret it; our embodied being makes our particular interpretation possible, an interpretation impossible to a different, lower kind of human being. Alamariu states, "The intellect is a purely physical quality like muscular strength." By becoming physically superior, we become intellectually superior. (The quadriplegic Stephen Hawking must have been an outlier.)

The Western world, like the ancient world, despises Bronze Age Males, and works to deprivilege, subjugate, and crush them whenever possible. Its leaders hatch conspiracies to control and subjugate everyone else. They rewrite history such that what we today recognize as objective historical fact is actually sophisticated modern myth. History rightly grasped is actually an account of the battles and triumphs of Bronze Age Males and their superior world.

In its place have emerged the "bugmen," who suppress the life-force and misdirect and pervert that natural energy into attacks on human superiority. These conspirators have crafted the calm, tranquil, egalitarian society of human rights, freedom within law, and equality of all humanity, including women. This is simply hatred for nature itself. BAM believes natural law should prevail everywhere, and that law, if observed, will lead to the ubiquitous superiority of beautiful young white muscular males. He writes, "youth and beauty are universally hated in all human societies in history. These societies are run by decrepit, sclerotic old men." What constitutes youth? Well, you are over the hill if you're in your 30s — middle-aged bodies nauseate nature. BAM counsels its young acolytes not to reason with their opponents (he laments the Western "development of logos and reason") but to ridicule them: "[M]ake the enemy look ridiculous ... dour, old, sclerotic, ugly, and pedantic," and never to underestimate the value of "a good prank."

One way the Bronze Age Males disrupt the current egalitarian regime is by capturing the spirit of cultural chaos — prostitutes, drug addicts, rapists, and murderers. The superior males must immerse themselves in the deepest depravity to tap into nature's power to sow chaos, which they must unleash to gain world control: "a whore puts cocaine on your tongue and you feel *true* power." They must spend time with this despised underclass, which manifests in suppressed form the genuine spirit of the life-force that has been marginalized by the Western egalitarian regime. "In your life," Alamariu declares, "you can break [the bug-men's] power and ascend to a chaos of joy and destruction."

Nihilism never sounded more delicious — the ecstasy of the destruction of everything, and the return to nature and natural law spawned by the impulse within society's most depraved.

The real world is not civilization and culture. The real world is uninhibited nature. The natural society is a "brotherhood of the free youths." There must be a "holy war" against the enemies of the youthful gods and their uninhibited life-force. Natural law must triumph.

BRONZE AGE POLITICS

BAM envisions a rigidly hierarchical social order with a certain kind of superior human (the Bronze Age Male) at the apex. But every social order implies a secondary yet important political order, and the Bronze Age political order coheres precisely with its social vision. It cannot be democratic, and by this BAM does not mean the sort of pure democracy that the Anglo-American tradition deplored, but, rather, precisely the sort of classically liberal order espoused by England and the United States and the modern West: the rule of law; constitutions and bills of rights; religious, political and economic liberty; negotiated politics; peaceful political transitions; and so forth. This classical liberalism leads to the egalitarian decadence we see around us, including ethnic heterogeneity. There is no way to create the BAM ethnostate without eliminating this Western, Christian-shaped constitutional democracy.

In the piratical world of the BAM, "the only right government is military government... We need warlord rule," Alamariu advises. And in actuality, the rationale for classical liberalism is just a conspiratorial veneer designed to cover up its own sordid will to power. The U.S. Founders, for example, were merely seeking "dominion and freedom of space to expand." They couldn't care less about a constitution, individual rights, free speech and press as they altruistically claimed. Like Nietzsche, BAM suggests that behind the curtain of every political rationale is the wizard imposing a will to power. While the most biblical political order possible in a fallen world is one of principled liberty and self-government within the bounds of law (ultimately God's law), the BAM political order is government by the young, beautiful, bodybuilding, sun-worshiping elite gods imposing their will on their inferiors. The only free citizens must be the governing pirate class.

THE BRONZE AGE MENTALITY
VERSUS CHRISTIANITY

BAM's conspiratorial view of history leads it to distrust Christian history. Actually, suggests Alamariu, Christianity likely began as paganism and was only later contorted into a theological system at the center of which rules a single deity imposing universal ethics. This was the nefarious work of Christian theologians and historians. Because of the instability and subjectivity of Christian history, argues Alamariu, "Christianity is a versatile faith, capable of many interpretations." Not that Christianity lacked any exhibition of paganism at all. Most Christian historians and theologians are ashamed (for example) of the conquistadors, but they, in fact, manifested the pagan life-force under the guise of the Christian faith. Still, Christian history in general is designed to crush the life-force in man. (This also was Nietzsche's take, by the way.)

By its very nature, therefore, BAM must repudiate the heart and soul of Christianity. The Bible is a texture of myths. Christ is not a hero because true heroes never sacrifice; they take territory. Man is not created in God's image, because there is no God to create anything. There is no creation. Matter is eternal. There is no resurrection, only reincarnation. Perhaps Alamariu's most explicitly anti-Christian tenet, however, is found in his statement that

> So much of this [monotheistic] story makes time a line and makes matter conditional on a deity or creator that lives outside it: the creation of matter out of nothing, the creation of your soul out of nothing. Matter is dead, and in some ways, homogeneous, and its meaning is "divine" only in the sense that it reveals the creation of the external deity, or even better, just the laws he made to govern. It seems and feels wrong, or runs against the immediate perception of the world, so it requires *faith*, a concept unknown to ancient pagans of all kinds. For this reason, the Romans considered Christians and Jews to be no different from atheists. (emphasis in original)

BAM is thoroughly existentialist. There is only this material world and what we (especially the Bronze Age Males) make of it. There can be no faith. WYSIAYG: What you see is all you get. And what you get is a divinized nature: there is no benevolent, sovereign Creator and Redeemer God behind it and working within it all.

But God's Word tells us that without faith, it is impossible to please God (Heb. 11:6). Therefore, BAM is blatantly contra-Christian. And the reason the imperial Romans considered Christians atheists is not because the Christians believed in faith, but because they repudiated all the false gods of the ancient world and demanded allegiance to the one true God.[5] In other words, the primitive Christians were considered atheists precisely because of their explicit repudiation of the kind of religion BAM is trying to revive.

THE BRONZE AGE MENTALITY
CHRISTIANS AND CONSERVATIVES

This contra-Christianity has not prevented BAM from influencing modern sociopolitical conservatism and conservative Christianity. Just as androgynous paganism has deeply infiltrated the Left, so Bronze Age paganism has influenced significant sectors of the Right, including the Christian Right. Matthew Continetti has shown how the New Right[6] has become suspiciously like the New Left in its statist lunge. The New Right is an influential, mostly younger segment of American conservatism convinced that the American Founding Protestant experiment of liberty under law has been a failure ("as momentous as this founding was, it is also where our current trouble began"[7]) and must be supplanted by a new conservative statism that crushes its Leftist

5   Larry W. Hurtado, *Destroyer of the Gods* (Waco, Texas: Baylor University Press, 2016), 37–76.

6   James M. Patterson, "Is the New Right Fascist?", *Religion & Liberty* [Summer 2003], 14–25.

7   Jason Michael Morgan, "The Pernicious Myth of 'Two Americas,'" *Chronicles*, October 2017, 12.

enemies by any means possible.[8] Continetti says:

> The first thing to say about the New Right is that it can get weird. Its ranks are composed almost entirely of men. They inhabit a social-media cocoon where they talk a lot about manhood, and strength, and manliness, and push-ups, and masculinity, and virility, and weight-lifting, and testosterone. "Wrestling should be mandated in middle schools," write Arthur Milikh and Scott Yenor in the [New Right] collection *Up from Conservatism*. "Students should learn to build and shoot guns as part of a normal course of action in schools and learn how to grow crops and prepare them for meals. Every male student should learn to skin an animal and every female to milk a cow."[9]

The influence of BAM is palpable, whether most in the New Right have read the book or not. The New Right is not simply opposed to sexual egalitarianism (as it should be). In addition, it advocates "muscular" politics, meaning the abandonment of the biblical idea of the rule of law applying to all equally, checks and balances on political power (since politicians, too, are depraved, even those on "our" side), and the state's role as limited to protecting life, liberty, and

8   Derek Suszko, "The Problem of Libertarianism," *The St. Croix Review*, Vol. LV, No. 4 [August/September 2022], 4–8.

9   Matthew Continetti, "The Left of the Right," https://www.commentary.org/articles/matthew-continetti/new-right-vs-conservatism/?fbclid=IwAR1dvXqqGBECuQCKivGb3E9PfJ-C140sQMH3HTwzMD9m-Wjv4LYs-997IALM_aem_ASWQgQFCU42Uamu1iPt4WV2TBzP-0oHCrgf-PuT9rACuFPtVzs22MJ_v3ay3Plr8qswg, accessed October 2, 2013.

property. The New Right wants to out-Left the Left at its political power game. Virtue is the exercise of coercive political power. Virtuous liberty be damned.

Conservative Christianity has not been spared the poison tentacles of BAM. A leading platform is the *American Reformer*, a cadre of youngish Protestants who blame the Protestant political philosophy of classical liberalism[10] (liberty under law) for the evils of modern culture. Human freedom leads to sin; therefore, freedom must be abolished. (Apparently God Himself was mistaken to give Adam and Eve free will in the garden.) Among the intellectual roots of the New Right is the BAM.

Christian Winter writes in *American Reformer* that young men are attracted to BAM because it offers a counter to the confines of modernity in its non-hierarchical, egalitarian order.[11] What we need is a modified vitalism, not BAM's pagan version, of course, but a revival of nature, which leads to human flourishing. We need to set before the eyes of young men not the heroes and gods of ancient Greece and Rome but Christian forefathers of masculine fortitude.

Winter argues that theory and theology are insufficient to persuade these young men. They need before their eyes muscular, masculine, overcoming Christian heroes they can emulate. The idea of enlisting Christian heroes is indeed a noble objective (just read Hebrews 11), but the quick,

10   David Conway, *Classical Liberalism* (New York: St. Martin's Press, 1995).

11   Christian Winter, "Towards a Christian Vitalism," *American Reformer* https://americanreformer.org/2023/05/towards-a-christian-vitalism/, May 15, 2023.

makeshift strategy of "Christian vitalism" in the face of
the popularity of BAM as the best way to appeal to young
men and forestall their gravitation to pagan vitalism is
what Francis Schaeffer called a "form of the world spirit."[12]
It seems a "seeker-sensitive" program for the 21st century
among the very people who would have derided Bill Hy-
bels and Rick Warren for fashioning an ideal faith to appeal to the unchurched "seekers." While correlation is not
causation, it is highly suspicious that "Christian vitalism"
just seemed magically to appear after, and as a consequence
of, BAM. And it would seem less selective or even disingen-
uous if its heroes included obese Christian intellectuals like
G. K. Chesterton, emaciated Christian prisoners like famed
Bulgarian pastor Haralan Popov, and urbane and modest
Christian poets like Gerard Manley Hopkins. I suspect,
however, that these mighty Christian men are not the sort
of male Christian heroes Winter has in mind.

This Christian-modified vitalism veers toward a new
syncretism, the attempted fusion of biblical faith and pagan
religion. If unchecked, it will be no less poisonous than the
syncretism of ancient Israel when it attempted to fuse bibli-
cal-covenantal faith to the religion of the surrounding pagan
nations. God abhors syncretism, and He sent his prophets
to both plead with Israel and fulminate against its apostasy.
Let us pray that "Christian Vitalism" reconsiders before it
walks itself into the syncretist camp.

Recently Jeffery J. Ventrella, Ezra Institute Senior Fellow
and noted Christian leader, posted on Facebook a remind-

---

12   Francis A. Schaeffer, *The Great Evangelical Disaster* (Westchester,
Illinois: Crossway, 1984), 111–140.

er to the young Christian masculinists talking so much about the necessity of weightlifting that physical fitness, while creditable, is not a fruit of the Spirit. I re-posted his statement. The pushback was swift and severe. One of the nation's young Christian masculinist leaders wrote privately begging me not to support this warning since I would alienate my audience of young men influenced by Christian masculinity (which, in reality, is the syncretistic "Christian Vitalism"). I responded that truth is truth and my interest has never been in avoiding offending a sector of my audience succumbing to sinful, worldly temptations.

It is, moreover, difficult to believe that Christian-modified vitalism has grappled with the issues surrounding how the Bible's teaching on masculinity (what of it there is; 95% of the Bible's commands are not sex-specific) applies in an informational and postindustrial world. The Bible's exhortations to and expectations of strength with reference to men are not arguments leveled against the sort of egalitarian and androgynous society presently afflicting the West. To argue as many conservatives today for the proper "roles" of men and women is to surrender the battle already. In the words of David Polansky:

> Once we acknowledge the need to establish masculine roles is more pressing than the need for masculinity itself, the cat's already out of the bag. We can argue, for example, that certain gender roles are salutary or desirable, but having admitted to ourselves that these are in fact roles, they necessarily lose their seriousness. It all becomes a kind of elaborate game. This is, incidentally,

why the "trad" [traditionalist] accounts one finds on social media [like BAM] have the feeling of camp. The men are caricatures of manliness, just as the women are caricatures of womanhood. They have the same uncanny feeling one gets from encountering AI.[13]

In God's creational world (even a fallen one not over-run by egalitarianism), masculinity is not a "role" to be recovered but a natural existence. How that looks in an age divinely blessed with labor-saving devices like automobiles and smart phones is not identical to how it looks in a premodern age that requires most men to skin a sheep for clothing, forge a wheel for transportation, or fell a tree for shelter. If it is necessary to revive an age that requires robust physical strength for everyday tasks, the Bible's authority and application are severely emaciated. The man's strength as a customer-serving warrior in the economy of contemporary culture and the wealth of free markets with which God has blessed the West, for example, is just as masculine as his strength had to be in premodern cultures. Assuming that the physical strength necessary for modern bricklayers is the sort young Christian men need to aspire to impoverishes the Bible's authority and dismisses vast areas of contemporary culture that require a different kind and measure of man's strength.

If young Christian men are seeking guidance in our apostate egalitarian age, they should start with the book of the Bible written specifically and explicitly to young men:

---

13 David Polansky, "No End of Men," *Washington Examiner*, October 3, 2023, 54.

the book of Proverbs. They are not called to recover masculinity; they are called to be godly men; nothing more, nothing less. Proverbs teaches that the true man is the man of God, and the man of God is the man of wisdom. Not a muscled physique but a righteous life is the mark of the true man. Care for the body is, of course, a biblical imperative since the body is the temple of the Holy Spirit (we must never be body-hating Gnostics). However, physical fitness is not a fruit of the Spirit, and if young males wish to become true men, they must begin with the fear of the Lord, not with a CrossFit regimen. This syncretistic adaptation of BAM to Christianity the book of Proverbs would identify as folly, whose end is destruction.

CONCLUSION

Opposition to the pervasive egalitarian, sociocultural regime of our time is a Christian imperative. Biblical Christianity is simply not compatible with sexual egalitarianism, but in Jerry Bowyer's metaphor, we cannot simply put the car in reverse; it is futile to traverse backwards on the road that led us to our present debacle in the first place. Rather, he suggests, we should do our best to "loop around" to get back to a biblically hierarchical time — which is by no means identical to a pagan anti-egalitarian time.

In this sense, we must be *non*-egalitarian, and not anti-egalitarian. Anti-egalitarianism carries in its bosom not just an aversion to the sexual egalitarianism of our time but also concessions both to the kind of thinking that got us here and to the battle tactics necessary to combat the present destination. In other words, anti-egalitarianism is a unique modern position possible only in the aftermath of egalitarian apostasy. It is not an older biblical non-egalitarianism. Although we cannot pretend as though the apostasy never occurred, we should do our best to restore the sort of thinking culturally prominent before egalitarianism came along. That certainly is not modern pagan anti-egalitarianism.

Non-egalitarianism is rooted in the creational order: recognition of men and women equally bearing God's image but created to fulfill diverse callings as they share the cultural mandate. The woman was made for the man and the man was not made for the woman, but the man knows he is incomplete without the woman, and knows that his very life is bound up in hers, just as hers is in his (1 Cor. 11:8–12). Therefore, he leads, and he doesn't dominate. Non-egalitarianism, therefore, is just as distant from the Christianized version of the Bronze Age Mindset (which is not the simple restoration of an ancient pagan way of thinking but rather the appropriation of that thinking to very unique, postmodern circumstances) as it is from modern apostate sexual egalitarianism.

Machismo and the misogyny it spawns are the marks of a mindset no less revolutionary than secular egalitarianism and the ideological feminism it exhibits. Both spring from rebellion against God's Word and Christ's Lordship. The destiny of apostate thinking is to swing incessantly between two or more poles of intellectual insurrection, assuming it can avoid one by adopting its opposite. In reality, all contra-biblical thinking is of the same species — man's rebellion against God and his revelation doomed for destruction and judgment apart from repentance.

Within the present secular egalitarian regime, the imperative of biblical Christians is to resist anti-egalitarianism (and its attendant Christianized version of the BAM) and work to restore non-egalitarianism. That restoration will equally restore truly biblical masculinity.

"THE MORE MELODIOUS MUSIC"
MUTUAL SOCIETY AND DUE BENEVOLENCE
IN PURITAN WRITINGS ON MARRIAGE
David Robinson

Genesis 2:18 sounds a discordant note in the narrative composition of Genesis 1-2. There is a refrain in Genesis 1. Six times we read "and God saw that it was good" (Gen. 1:4,10,12,18,21,24) with an additional "and behold, it was very good" (Gen. 1:30), announcing the complete goodness of God's creation.[1] But then we read in Genesis 2:18: "It's not good for the man to be alone; I will make a helper fit for him."

The LORD God brings every beast from the field and every bird of the heavens to the man, to see what he will call them (Gen. 2:19). The man is given dominion. He names the animals. So far, so good. But then the narrative turns back to what is not good, "for Adam there was not found a helper fit for him" (Gen. 2:20).

Having read Genesis 1, we already know that there will be male and female and we already know that God bless-

---

1   Quotations from Scripture are from the *English Standard Version* (Crossway, 2016).

es them and commands them to be fruitful and multiply (Gen. 1:26-28). The union of man and woman is prolific, and children are one of the good ends of marriage. What we did not know reading Genesis 1 was that between the sixth "good" and the seventh "very good" there was a "not good." The blessing and command to be fruitful and multiply follows the divine resolution to the "not good" of being alone. God caused the man to fall into a deep sleep and took from his side and built a woman, a helper fit for the man, and brought her to the man. It is for this reason that "a man shall leave his father and his mother and hold fast to his wife, and they shall become one flesh" (Gen. 2:24).

Yes, the union of man and wife is prolific, and children are one of the good ends of marriage, but it was not good for the man to be alone and his union and mutual society with his wife is another good end of marriage. God did not announce his "very good" judgment on creation until he instituted and ordained the marriage of husband and wife.

Mutual society and children are two ends (or causes) of marriage, which God ordained in Genesis 1-2. There is a third cause, which the Apostle Paul identifies in 1 Corinthians 7:1, "because of the temptation to sexual immorality, each man should have his own wife and each woman her own husband."

The Form of Solemnization of Matrimony in the Book of Common Prayer (1662) lists the causes for which marriage was ordained in the following order:

First, it was ordained for the procreation of children, to be brought up in the fear and nurture of the Lord, and to the praise of his holy Name.

Secondly, it was ordained for a remedy against sin, and to avoid fornication; that such persons as have not the gift of celibacy might marry, and keep themselves undefiled members of Christ's body.

Thirdly, it was ordained for the mutual society, help, and comfort, that the one ought to have of the other, both in prosperity and adversity.[2]

Mutual society is placed third; however, as we have seen, in Genesis 1-2 it precedes the cause of children by first resolving the "not good" of man being alone and bringing creation to its sevenfold goodness. Mutual society comes first, then children. As it was in Genesis, so it is in every godly marriage, by at least 9 months.

The Puritans of the sixteenth and seventeenth centuries recognized the traditional three causes of marriage which are listed in the Book of Common Prayer; however, they placed greater emphasis on the cause of mutual society and frequently reversed the order of the causes when preaching on marriage.[3] Of the three causes, mutual society seems the least concerned with the sexual union; however, the Puritans saw the marriage bed as vital to the mutual society of husband and wife. In this chapter, I want to review various Puritan sermons on marriage from the sixteenth

---

2   *The Book of Common Prayer 1662 Version*, Everyman's Library (London: Everyman Publishers, 1999), 300.

3   James Johnson, *A Society Ordained by God: English Puritan Marriage Doctrine in the First Half of the Seventeenth Century* (Nashville: Abingdon Press, 1970), 22, 42, 58, 68, 95-96, 100, 114, 126, 173.

and seventeenth centuries and highlight their preaching on mutual society and sexual intimacy, which they called "due benevolence."

H.L. Mencken famously defined Puritanism as "the haunting fear that someone, somewhere may be happy."[4] This comment is the epitome of caricature. That the Puritans were happy is obvious to anyone who read them. Reading them makes me happy, not fleetingly or superficially, but really happy. Their sermons on marriage are not entirely joyful. They are didactic and practical, with lots of instruction on domestic duties, which when heeded, makes for a joyful marriage and home. Their sermons are not entirely joyful, but they are designed for a joyful marriage.

CHOOSING A SPOUSE

A key factor in whether a marriage will be joyful may depend on whether a spouse is well-chosen, and the Puritans gave advice for choosing a spouse. Henry Smith (ca. 1550-1591) warns against choosing a spouse for gentry, riches, or beauty.[5] Adam was in a deep sleep while God prepared a wife for him. Smith observes a lesson in Adam's sleep for those choosing a spouse. His sleep "teaches us our

---

4   H.L. Mencken and George Jean Nathan, "Clinical Notes," *The American Mercury* 4, no.13: 59, column 1.

5   Henry Smith, *A Preparative to Marriage. The Summe Whereof Was Spoken at a Contract and Inlarged after* (London, 1591), 10 (available online: http://name.umdl.umich.edu/A12367.0001.001.) Cf. William Secker, *A Wedding Ring Fit for the Finger, or The salve of Divinity on the Sore of Humanity: Laid Open in a Sermon at a Wedding in Edmonton* (London, 1658), 49-53 (available online: http://name.umdl.umich.edu/A92800.0001.001).

affections, our lusts, and our concupiscence should sleep while we go about this action."[6]

What then are the criteria? A potential spouse must not only be in the Lord and virtuous, but suitable and fit. Compatibility matters. Smith sees a symbol of suitability in the wedding ring, which "neither pincheth, nor slippeth."[7] Just as God sought a king after his own heart, so a man should seek a wife after his own heart.

THE DUTY OF LOVE

Marriage is a covenant, a relationship of mutual belonging, not just a legal union but a union of hearts. William Secker (d. 1681) describes this concord: "Husband and wife should be like two candles burning together, which makes the house more lightsome, or like two fragrant flowers bound up in one nosegay that augments its sweetness; or like two well-tuned instruments, which sounding together, makes the more melodious music."[8] Faithful love makes the mutual society of husband and wife melodious.

The Puritans are most moving when writing and preaching on the duty of love. Smith calls love the cardinal virtue of marriage. A magistrate must have justice, the preacher must have knowledge, the soldier must have fortitude, and a marriage must have love.[9] William Gouge (1575-1653) writes that the hearts of husband and wife must be "knit to-

---

6   Smith, *A Preparative to Marriage*, 10. I have modernized the spelling in my quotations throughout.

7   Smith, *A Preparative to Marriage*, 31.

8   Secker, *A Wedding Ring Fit for the Finger*, 33.

9   Smith, *A Preparative to Marriage*, 55.

gether by a true, spiritual, matrimonial love: always delighting one in another, ever helpful one to another, and ready with all willingness and cheerfulness to perform all those duties which they owe one to another."[10]

William Whately (1583-1639) defines spiritual and matrimonial love. Spiritual love is "grounded principally upon the commandment of God that requires it, not upon the face, favour, proportion, beauty, dowry, nobility, gifts or goods parts of him or her to whom it is due ... spiritual love, that looks upon God, rests upon his will, yields to his commandment, and resolves to obey it."[11] Spiritual love is spousal love whose source and sustenance is our love of God, expressed by our obedience to his commandments.

Matrimonial love is "the nuptial love of yoke-fellows.... It is the fixing of their hearts in the good liking each of other, as the only fit and good match that could be found under the sun for them."[12] How do you attain and grow in this love? Whately counsels married couples to "take special notice of God's gracious providence, for good in their match. They which look to God as the match-maker, and that in favour take each other as love-tokens from heaven, and therefore cannot but love that well, which comes as a sign of his favour, whom they strive to love above all.... He that loves the giver, will love the gift also."[13] God's love for

---

10   William Gouge, *Domestical Duties*, II.2.19 (available online: https://www.chapellibrary.org/pdf/books/otddu1.pdf).

11   William Whately, *A Bride-bush, or A wedding Sermon Compendiously Describing the Duties of Married Persons* (London, 1617), 7 (available online: http://name.umdl.umich.edu/A14989.0001.001).

12   Whately, *A Bride-bush*, 8.

13   Whately, *Bride-bush*, 11.

us is the source and sustenance of marital love.

Spiritual and marital love unites the hearts of husband and wife. Scripture and prayer are vital to such loving concord. Whately exhorts, "Pray together one with and for another in secret; confer, read the Word of God together, and sing Psalms alone: this will so rivet your hearts, that no contention shall dissever them."[14]

DUE BENEVOLENCE

Scripture and prayer not only keep the flame of love burning, they keep the flame of love holy. Whately applies 1 Timothy 4:4-5 to the marriage bed: "For everything created by God is good, and nothing is to be rejected if it is received with thanksgiving, for it is made holy by the word of God and prayer." The marriage bed is sanctified and used reverently with prayer and thanksgiving.[15]

Such sanctity and reverence preserve the marriage bed from corruption of lust. Love edifies, sustains, and keeps boundaries; lust destroys, corrupts, and breaks boundaries. Alexander Niccholes warns that lust is "the Spring-frost of beauty, the tyrant of the night, the enemy of the day, the most potent match-maker in all marriages under thirty, and the chief breaker of all from eighteen to eighty."[16] For the Puritans, unchecked lust not only leads to adultery, it corrupts genuine love within the marriage: "Men and women

---

14   Whately, *Bride-bush*, 10.

15   Whately, *Bride-bush*, 43.

16   Alexander Niccholes, *A Discourse of Marriage and Wiving and of the Greatest Mystery therein Contained* (London, 1615), 30 (available online: http://name.umdl.umich.edu/A08179.0001.001).

must not come together as brute creatures and unreasonable beasts, through the heat of desire."[17] The sexual union is a union of holy love, not brute desire.

Holy love is not grave, but cheerful. Whately counsels the bride and groom concerning their "matrimonial meeting": "First, it must be cheerful: they must lovingly, willingly and familiarly communicate themselves unto themselves, which is the best means to continue and nourish their mutual natural love, and by which the true and proper ends of matrimony shall be attained in best manner."[18] Note the adverbs: cheerful, lovingly, willingly, and familiarly. William Gouge describes sexual intimacy as pure, fervent, proper, and essential:

> that husband and wife mutually delight each in other, and maintain a pure and fervent love betwixt themselves, yielding that due benevolence one to another which is warranted and sanctified by God's word, and ordained of God for this particular end. This due benevolence (as the Apostle styleth it) is one of the most proper and essential acts of marriage: and necessary for the main and principal ends thereof: as for preservation of chastity in such as have not the gift of continency, for increasing the world with a legitimate brood, and for linking the affections of the married couple more firmly together.[19]

---

17   Whately, *A Bride-bush*, 43.

18   Whately, *A Bride-bush*, 43.

19   Gouge, *Domestical Duties*, II.2.9.

Sexual intimacy maintains a pure and fervent love and links the affections of husband and wife more firmly together.

Finally, the Puritans set criteria for times of abstinence. For Whately, "nuptial meetings must be seasonable and at lawful times."[20] He then offers a fairly detailed excursus on menstruation, in the midst of which he tells the congregation (this is a wedding sermon!): "Bear then with necessary plainness. And let no women grieve that the cause of her fruitfulness is known."[21] Gouge lists three reasons for abstaining: when the performance of due benevolence is against piety (times of prayer and fasting), against mercy (e.g., when a spouse is sick), or against modesty (i.e., during menstruation).[22]

Of the three causes of marriage, the Puritans elevated the mutual society of husband and wife. Children are raised in the love and stability of this mutual society and sexual intimacy links the affections of husband and wife more firmly within this mutual society. The marriage bed is holy, sanctified by prayer and thanksgiving, but it is also cheerful and delightful. The mutual love of husband and wife is sustained and nourished when they "look to God as the match-maker, and that in favour take each other as love-tokens from heaven" and so "lovingly, willingly and familiarly communicate themselves unto themselves."[23]

---

20 Whately, *A Bride-bush*, 44.
21 Whately, *A Bride-bush*, 44.
22 Gouge, *Domestical Duties*, II.2.9.
23 Whately, *A Bride-bush*, 11, 43.

THE BIBLICAL FAMILY IDEAL
Willem J. Ouweneel

BAD FAMILIES IN THE BIBLE

Writing about the biblical family ideal is not so straightforward as might be assumed, because the Bible hardly presents us with an explicit description of such an ideal. On the contrary, we encounter many families in the Bible that are not ideal at all, to say the least, and such right from the beginning. Of Adam and Eve's first two sons, the eldest killed the second one (Gen. 4). One of Noah's three sons, Ham, dishonored his own father (Gen. 9). The patriarch Abraham had various wives—which was a bad start in the first place—and had sons from these wives, Ishmael and Isaac, who had a bad relationship (Gen. 21:8–11). Isaac had twin sons, Esau and Jacob, who had a strained relationship, too; mother Rebekah supported Jacob, and Isaac supported Esau (Gen. 28). Jacob had twelve sons from four wives and concubines, among whom he favored his eleventh son, Joseph—understandably but unwisely—which led to harsh and long-lasting consequences: Joseph was rejected and sold by his older brothers (Gen. 37).

Moses was almost killed because he failed in his fa-

therhood, having neglected to circumcise his youngest
son (Ex. 4:24–26). The judge Gideon had seventy sons
because he had many wives; one of them killed almost all
the other sons (Jdg. 9). The priest Eli had two sons, Hoph-
ni and Phinehas, evil men who made a mockery of their
priesthood; this was Eli's own fault because he had failed
to 'restrain' (or, rebuke) them (1 Sam. 3:13). The prophet
Samuel unwisely favored his two unrighteous sons (1 Sam.
8:1–3). King David, by his own fault, met with great quar-
rels among his sons, which cost the lives of several of them:
Amnon, Absalom (2 Sam. 13–16), later also Adonijah (1
Kings 1). King Solomon had many heathen wives, whose
idols he began to serve, thus setting a bad example to his
children (1 Kings 11).

Besides this, there are other exceptions to the rule of
the "normal" family. I am referring to situations in which
the compulsion to have children could be so great that, in
certain cases, a replacement or surrogate mom or dad had
to be found. On the one hand, this could mean that a man
took a bondwoman to have children from her who were
counted as children of his barren wife; Abraham and Hagar
were an unhappy example of this. On the other hand,
there was the levirate marriage, in which a widow married
a brother or close relative of her deceased husband, to have
children from him who were counted as children of her
deceased husband; Boaz and Ruth were a happy example of
this. Only of a few of the later kings of the two tribes (the
kingdom of Judah) is it said that they did what was "right in
the eyes of the LORD," such as Asa, Joash (in the beginning),
Amaziah ("yet not with a whole heart"), Uzziah (although

he badly fell in the end), Jotham, Hezekiah, and Josiah. It has been suggested that, especially if the fathers were wicked kings, the mothers must have played an essential role in the education of these righteous sons. With honor, we mention two of them: Hezekiah's mother was Abijah, a daughter of Zechariah (2 Chron. 29:1; possibly this was Zechariah the priest, 2 Chron. 24:20–22; 26:5), and Josiah's mother was Jedidah, a daughter of Adaiah of Boskath (2 Kings 22:1). In fact, we do not know anything of these mothers, but they are the best candidates for the positive influence that these kings must have undergone in their early youth.

Is there any truly harmonious family that could be pointed out in the Bible? Perhaps the family of Elkanah and Hannah (in the end, they had six children, with a very special eldest son: Samuel, see 1 Sam. 1)? Or the prophet Isaiah and his wife and two sons (Is. 8)? Or the family of the priest Zechariah and Elizabeth, an elderly couple with just one son (Luke 1)? Or the family of Joseph and Mary, (even if she had difficulty understanding her eldest son (Luke 2:48; John 2:1–5)? Or do we simply know too little of these families to find out if they matched the biblical family ideal?

PROCREATION

If we wish to discover the contours of the ideal biblical family, let us look not for good biblical examples but rather for good biblical *principles*. It is quite interesting to see what was the very first divine commandment that we find in the Bible: "Be fruitful and multiply and fill the earth" (Gen. 1:28). If a person cannot find an appropriate husband or wife, or a couple turns out to be barren, this commandment cannot be fulfilled in its primary sense (apart from possibilities such as the adoption of children, or a spiritual "parenthood," for instance, for younger people in one's congregation). But apart from this, the commandment stands till this very day. I have difficulty believing the sincerity and conviction of couples who, because of their "ministry" or otherwise, decide to lead a married life but refrain from having children. It is the normal way for any person desiring to live according to the Bible to marry and have children. If the first commandment is, "Be fruitful and multiply," the commandment preceding this one is this: "a man shall leave his father and his mother [thus setting up a new social unit] and hold fast to his wife [which presupposes a wedding], and they shall become one flesh" (Gen. 2:24)—in that order.

In this respect, notice the following interesting differences between Genesis 1 and 2. In Genesis 1 we read, "God created man in his own image…, male and female he created them" (v. 27). God created humanity in two "editions," the male and the female, and he blessed the sexual differences between the two in order that children would be procreated by them. As a consequence, the earth would be 'filled" with *many* males and females, all with the same duty: finding an appropriate partner, and having children together.

In Genesis 2, the situation is quite different. Here, there is no mention of children at all. It is rather the *correspondence* and *attraction* between the two sexes that are emphasized. The Lord said, "It is not good that the man should be alone; I will make him a helper fit for [or, corresponding to] him" (Gen. 2:18). After Eve had been formed out of the side of Adam, the latter said (v. 23), "This at last is bone of my bones and flesh of my flesh; she shall be called Woman [Hebrew *Ishah*], because she was taken out of Man [Hebrew *Ish*]." Man and Woman are each other's counterparts; they correspond to each other, and they complete each other. The unity and harmony between the two are vital elements of the biblical family ideal because it creates the right atmosphere for the kids' education; this ideal cannot be realized if husband and wife do not display at least a fair dose of such concord.

In Genesis 1, sexual unity is the means of being fruitful and multiplying. But in Genesis 2, sexual unity ("becoming one flesh") is, first of all, the means of physically expressing the love between husband and wife (children not being mentioned; compare the Song of Solomon). Please note that these two aspects should be kept together: "What God has joined together, let not man separate' (Matt. 19:6). That is, in the biblical ideal, sexual unity is never for procreation *only*, but neither is it an expression of love *only*. The two belong together: procreation is rooted in the love and harmony of a husband and wife. To put it this way: in a biblical family, children should be made aware of the fact that they were born out of the love of mom and dad.

EDUCATION

Having borne children, parents are now responsible for educating them. The purpose of the biblical family is to be a warm nest of godly love, harmony and safety, in which children are raised to become spiritually healthy, balanced, and above all godly adults. This demands biblical education: "Fathers, bring your children up in the discipline and instruction of the Lord" (Eph. 6:4). "Discipline" means: learn to follow his rules; 'instruction" means: learn who and what he *is*.

This is in line with the words of Moses: "these words that I command you today shall be on your heart. You shall teach them diligently to your children, and shall talk of them when you sit in your house, and when you walk by the way, and when you lie down, and when you rise" (Deut. 6:6–7). And after Paul and Moses, listen to Asaph: "I will utter…things that we have heard and known, that our fathers have told us. We will not hide them from their children, but tell to the coming generation the glorious deeds of the Lord, and his might, and the wonders that he has done" (Ps. 78:2–4, 6; cf. 22:30; 48:13). Children, learn what the Lord was and is, what he did and does, then you will better understand what he expects from *you*.

Teaching children the things of God is first and foremost a matter of *example*. The godly behavior of believing parents is far more important than the things they say, and is, partly unconsciously, noticed much more keenly by children than all their good words. Take the example of Ezra: "Ezra had set his heart to study the Law of the Lord, and to do it and to teach his statutes and rules in Israel" (Ezra 7:10)—in this order: first studying, then putting into practice what you have studied, and only then teaching these things to others, in this case your children.

Right in the beginning of Israel's history as a nation, in the book of Exodus, the great emphasis on educating children is remarkable. They must learn to see what is going on in the world in the light of God (10:1–2). The unity of the family in the service of God is underlined (10:8–11). There is the light of the Lamb in the family within a dark world (10:23; the Lamb was taken into the family just before the plague of darkness, 12:3). There is the lesson that, by nature, all children are under God's judgment (11:5–7). For four days, the entire family was focusing upon the Lamb (12:3–7). Then there was the important lesson that the children of God's people were safe behind the blood of the Lamb (12:11–15), and, more generally, the teaching on the significance of *Pesach* (the Passover) (12:24–27) and of *Matsot* (the feast of the unleavened loaves; 13:4–10; cf. 1 Cor. 5:7–8), and of the consecration of the firstborn (13:11–16).

The Torah pays great attention to the questions that are asked by children and should be taken very seriously by the parents, even if they are silly or simple. In the Jewish tradition of the *Pesach* meal, the following four questions are asked:

(a) The *wise* child asks this extensive question: "What is the meaning of the testimonies and the statutes and the rules that the LORD our God has commanded you?" (Deut. 6:20)—and gets an extensive answer.

(b) The *bad* child asks, "What does this service mean to *you*?" (as several translations render it in Ex. 12:26)—thus excluding himself from the matter. The child is curious, but hesitates to be part of what is going on.

(c) The *simple* child only asks, "What is this?" (as several translations render it in Ex. 13:14)—and gets an extensive answer, too.

(d) The *ignorant* child does not yet know how to ask questions, and nonetheless receives an answer (Ex. 13:8).

GOD AND HIS CHILDREN

In the biblical family, both parents play important roles in teaching their children the rules of biblical life. King Solomon tells the child this: "Hear, my son, your *father's* instruction, and forsake not your *mother's* teaching, for they are a graceful garland for your head and pendants for your neck" (Prov. 1:8–9). And further down: "My son, keep your *father's* commandment, and forsake not your *mother's* teaching. Bind them on your heart always; tie them around your neck. When you walk, they will lead you; when you lie down, they will watch over you; and when you awake, they will talk with you. For the commandment is a lamp and the teaching a light, and the reproofs of discipline are the way of life" (6:20–23). The Hebrew word for "teaching" here is *torah*, which is also the word for "law" (literally, Teaching), the Law of the Lord.

This takes us to the important point of God's own "family." The biblical family (godly parents and children) is modeled after God's family. He called Israel his "firstborn son" (Ex. 4:22), and in the plural: "You are the sons of the LORD your God' (Deut. 14:1), "children of the living God" (Hos. 1:10). Just as the mother in Proverbs teaches her children *torah*, God teaches his children *Torah*—not as harsh, unpleasant rules (a heavy "yoke," Acts 15:10), but as their "very life" (Deut. 32:47), the air they breathe, the food they eat, the milk they drink.

God dealt with the Israelites as his "children," although he knew very well that many of his people had no (or, not yet any) vital relationship with him. Allow me to apply this as follows: believing parents ought not to deal with their children as "pagans" until they are "converted" (as seems to be the case in some Christian denominations), but rather deal with them as children of God until, sadly, the opposite comes to light very clearly. As I quoted from Ephesians 6, children should be raised in the discipline and instruction of the Lord.

It is important to understand this. In the strict sense, the Church of God is "a holy congregation and gathering of true Christian believers" (Belgic Confession Art. 27); this is a company of Christian *individuals*. But the Kingdom of God, or the New Covenant, is a matter of believers *together with their children*. The Kingdom and the Covenant are *family* matters. This is why Jesus said, "Let the children come to me; do not hinder them, for *to such belongs the kingdom of God*" (Mark 10:14). And the apostle Paul said that, if at least one of the parents is a Christian, then the children are "holy" (set apart from the world, and consecrated to God, 1 Cor. 7:14), even if they, as yet, have not demonstrated any determination of personally following Christ. Therefore, God made his covenant not only with Abraham but also with the latter's "offspring" (Gen. 17:9). In the context of the New Covenant (Jer. 31:31–34), we read, "Their children shall be as they were of old, and their congregation shall be established before me" (30:20); and further down: "I will give them one heart and one way, that they may fear me forever, for their own good *and the good of their children after them.* I will make with them an everlasting covenant, that I will not turn away from doing good to them. And I will put the fear of me in their hearts, that they may not turn from me" (32:39–40).

Some of us may stress the covenant aspect a little more, I like to stress the kingdom aspect a little more. But for our present purpose, the net result is the same. God's relationships with his people are never strictly individual; God thinks in terms of families: If there is "a feast to the Lord," we "go with our sons and daughters" (Ex. 10:9). If God has anything good to give away, it "is for you *and for your children*" (Acts 2:39).

This is the great message that believing parents may tell their children: The Lord has granted mom and dad something fantastic: they are children of God, they have eternal life, eternal salvation, and are on their way to eternal bliss—*but God intended these same things for their children.* God did not give the children to their parents in order that they would get lost—although this would happen if they would consciously and permanently turn their back to him—but in order that they would receive the same blessings that the parents, by grace, have received from God.

This is what the biblical family is: it is a place where children are led into the sphere of blessings that their parents are already familiar with. It is a place where the children bless their parents for this (cf. Prov. 31:28). A place where parents earnestly pray for their children (cf. Job 1:5). A place where each parent says, "as for me and my house, we will serve the LORD" (Josh. 24:15), and, "I have no greater joy than to hear that my children are walking in the truth" (3 John 1:4). A place where the word is heard, "Be careful to obey all these words that I command you, that it may go well with you and with your children after you forever, when you do what is good and right in the sight of the LORD your God" (Deut. 12:28).

www.ingramcontent.com/pod-product-compliance
Lightning Source LLC
Chambersburg PA
CBHW071008120626
46546CB00003B/993